Pope John Paul II
A Remarkable Life

Pope John Paul II - a Remarkable Life

produced in collaboration with The Universe Catholic weekly
1st Floor St. James's Buildings, Oxford Street, Manchester M1 6FP

Editor: Joseph Kelly
Design and Production: Brendan Gilligan
Research: James Kelly and Lynda Walker
Photographs: Catholic News Service, Washington,
and The Press Association, London

The stranger from a far off land who taught us to live like Christ

Shortly after 9.37pm on Saturday, 2nd April 2005, Our Lord bent down to lift the cross of the sufferings of this world from the shoulders of Karol Wojtyla, Pope John Paul II. After one of the most remarkable papacies of all time, our beloved pontiff finally succumbed to a combination of physical frailties that had broken his body, but never his spirit. John Paul II lived in both the shadow and the light of the Cross, modelling his life on the person of Christ and, in his final hours, sharing with the world a very public suffering.

We never will see the likes of Wojtyla again. From humble origins in Wadowice, Poland, he rose to become the 263rd successor of St. Peter as bishop of Rome and supreme pastor of the universal church. He chose as his motto the words *Totus Tuus, All for You*, offering everything to be ministered through the hands of Mary for the glory of God. In this he imitated Mary's twofold vocation: to bring Christ into the world and then to return him to the world to challenge the secular culture at every turn. From the moment of his election he lived out that remarkable commitment to service that challenged the world with the message of the cross – the message of Good Friday and Easter – until the end.

Long before he became pope, Karol Wojtyla was developing a philosophy that he called 'personalism', a radical interpretation of the Christian message that put the individual person at the centre of the human drama – "the work is for the man, and not man for the work," he wrote.

Brought up under the yoke of Nazism, and then communism, Wojtyla sensed that true liberation of the spirit came not from subscription to any socio-economic or political system, but to the recognition of the intrinsic dignity of every single person. It was this single thought that came to dominate his papacy, and to condition his every response to human situations. It brought him into direct conflict with all forms of dictatorship, encouraging workers' rights across the world, and bringing about the collapse of the Soviet Socialist Republic, and a monumental change in the Cold War.

Pope John Paul II was always pastoral and sensitive to the feelings of each individual he met, but there was an iron fist concealed in his velvet glove. His unshakable will always fought for the dignity of every human person from conception to death. In this effort, he changed the way the world values the dignity of the individual.

At a personal level he brought a philosopher's intellect, a pilgrim's spiritual intensity and an actor's flair for the dramatic, a combination that made him one of the most forceful moral leaders of the modern age. A consummate communicator, he was the first pope of the media age, and the most travelled in history, taking his message to 129 countries in 104 trips outside Italy. In guiding the Catholic Church into the third millennium, John Paul II placed Catholicism on both the international political stage, and at the forefront of the global moral agenda.

He spoke with intensity and passion on a wide range of contemporary issues, but above all, his message was one of the liberating joy that lies at the heart of the Catholic faith.

"Christ came to bring joy," he said, "joy to children, joy to parents, joy to families and friends, joy to workers and scholars, joy to the sick and elderly, joy to all humanity. In a true sense joy is the keynote message of Christianity and the recurring motif of the Gospels. Go therefore and become messengers of joy."

In the midst of the sadness of losing one so loved, that's the message he'd like us to remember.

Joseph Kelly

Editorial Director:
Gabriel Communications Ltd

Editor:
The Universe Catholic weekly
Catholic Life
Who's Who in Catholic Life

Reflections on a unique papacy

When Pope John Paul II celebrated 25 years in office in October 2003, the world took stock of a pontificate that had already helped shape political events, set new directions for the Catholic Church and offered spiritual inspiration to millions of people around the globe.

By any measure, this was a papacy for the ages. Since his election on the 16th October, 1978, Pope John Paul delivered more speeches, met with more world leaders, canonised more saints and kissed more babies than any previous pontiff. Visiting 129 countries, he implemented the Church's own form of globalisation.

And in more than 50 major documents, on themes ranging from economics to the Rosary, he brought the Gospel and Church teachings to bear on nearly every aspect of modern life.

As his passing is mourned, everyone agrees this Pope has left a massive moral legacy, inside and outside the Church.

"The Pope has an important message to deliver, and people are listening — perhaps more than ever," said Vatican spokesman Joaquin Navarro-Valls at the time of the Pope's 25th election anniversary. "He is the only global leader who is worried about the spiritual well-being of today's men and women, as opposed to their material well-being. He asks, 'Who are you?' instead of 'What do you want to do?' or 'What do you want to buy?' And people understand this and respond to it," he said.

At the start of the 21st century, a time of rapid changes in technology and biology, the Pope drew closer to this dominant theme, Navarro-Valls said.

For papal biographer George Weigel, the Pope had a tremendous impact on the world and the Church precisely because

"He's been the great Christian witness of our time, the man who has most persuasively embodied the liberating power of Christian faith. That had concrete, measurable political results in east-central Europe in the revolution of 1989; but it has also had an immeasurable impact on innumerable lives throughout the world," said Weigel.

Many at the Vatican now believe that the Pope's infirmities in later years added a new dimension to his message.

"When the Mass was celebrated by someone in his condition, the sacrifice of Christ became even more evident," said Cardinal Jozef Tomko, a long-time friend and retired Vatican official.

"What came through was a deep spirituality and the acceptance of his limitations. I think in those conditions he was winning even more people to Christ than before."

The first non-Italian pontiff in 455 years, Pope John Paul II declared early on that the Second Vatican Council had set his agenda. In particular, his global ministry quickly focused on Vatican II's engagement of modern culture.

At the teaching level, the Pope penned three major encyclicals on economic and social justice issues and addressed the rich-poor imbalance continent-by-continent in post-synodal documents. Over his last 10 years, he also authored three other encyclicals that strongly challenged what he saw as a prevailing moral relativism in post-modern society. *Veritatis Splendour* spoke of the truth of the Church's moral teachings, *Evangelium Vitae* defended the inviolability of human life against what the Pope called a "culture of death," and *Fides et Ratio* argued that human reason cannot be detached from faith in God.

Meanwhile, under his guidance, Vatican agencies issued important instructions on such specific questions as foreign debt, in vitro fertilisation, the arms industry, the role of the mass media and the impact of the Internet.

Through all these pronouncements ran a central theme: that freedom becomes destructive when people forget they are created in God's image. Whether an unborn child or an impoverished African, the Pope said, every human being has a value that goes beyond earthly advantages and accomplishments.

While pushing Catholic teaching into virtually every area of modern life, the Pope also took the measure of the Church's past mistakes. At his insistence, the Church acknowledged historical errors in condemning 16th-century astronomer Galileo Galilei, in participating in European religious wars, and even in its missionary approach in some New World territories.

Against considerable resistance within his own Vatican hierarchy, the Pope commissioned critical studies on the Church's role in the Inquisition and the Crusades and on the failings of Christians during the Holocaust.

On an interreligious level, Pope John Paul reached out in ways that were once considered impossible or even heretical. In 1986, he visited a Jewish synagogue in Rome, then in 2000 prayed at the Western Wall in Jerusalem — a gesture that won the hearts of many Jews worldwide.

In Syria, he became the first Pope to visit a mosque, and in Morocco he spoke to thousands of cheering Muslim youths.

Twice he convened leaders of other religions and other Churches for prayer meetings in Assisi, where participants denounced all acts of war and terrorism carried out in the name of religion.

Within the Church, the Pope was no less dynamic. He disciplined dissenting theologians, promulgated a new Code of Canon Law, issued new directives calling for clearer Catholic identity in Church universities, and defended with the full weight of his authority the Church's all-male priesthood.

Some critics said that in dealing with Church problems, the Pope's management style was too detached. They cited the clerical sex abuse crisis as an example of where the pontiff should have called bishops and others to closer accountability.

Vatican officials rejected that criticism, pointing out that the Pope several times pronounced prophetically against sex abuse and other moral failings by Church ministers. The Pope's job was not to pore over dossiers but to set clear directions, they said.

"This was not a pontificate that acted in a crisis management style. He went beyond crisis management, to the root of the problem. And in the case of sex abuse, the real problem was in formation," said Navarro-Valls, the Vatican spokesman.

As a teacher of the Faith, the Pope was exhaustive, demanding and authoritative. The Catechism of the Catholic Church was his longest document, and will no doubt be seen as one of the great accomplishments of this pontificate.

The Pope brooked no dissent among the faithful, and in a 1998 document he invoked penalties against Catholics who rejected the Church's wide range of "definitive" positions, including those on human sexuality. That prompted criticism by some groups of laity and theologians, especially in Europe and the United States. Such groups said the Pope presided over an excessive centralisation of Church power and authority at the expense of local churches. While supporting Vatican II's promotion of the laity in the Church, the Pope warned against confusing the roles of lay Catholics and ordained priests.

He supported clerically managed lay organisations like Opus Dei, which grew in influence. As opposed to models of power-sharing in the Church, Pope John Paul proposed models of holiness to the world's 1.1 billion Catholics. He canonised more than 470 people from dozens of countries and beatified more than 1,300 – including the first lay couple.

The Pope's record on ecumenism contained a long list of agreements, joint declarations and mutual gestures of good will, especially with some ancient Eastern churches. But as common ground was staked out among the Churches, the remaining obstacles stood in even higher relief. The Vatican's clear injunction against shared Eucharist with Protestant churches may have seemed arbitrary to critics, but the Pope viewed it as a painful reminder of the distance yet to be travelled in ecumenical dialogue.

Over later years, relations with the Russian Orthodox Church sharply deteriorated as a result of the Pope's determination to rebuild Catholic communities in Russia and other parts of Eastern Europe. Surely one of the Pope's biggest disappointments was the failure to visit Moscow, which he would undertake only with the Orthodox Church's blessing.

Pope John Paul, perhaps, more than any of his predecessors, shaped the hierarchy in his image. He named more than three quarters of the world's active bishops and 96 per cent of the cardinals who will elect his successor.

During his papacy, the Church expanded greatly in Africa and made significant advances in Asia and Oceania. This distinctly Third World tilt was spotlighted during the Pope's more than 100 foreign trips, when he used local customs in his liturgies, spoke the native language and praised indigenous writers and thinkers.

But the trips had enormous missionary objectives as well.

While respectful of the non-Catholic or non-Christian majorities along his itinerary, the Pope always presented the figure of Christ and the Gospel message to any and all of his listeners.

That was in keeping with the Pope's conviction that while all people can be saved, Christ is the unique Saviour for all people – a point made forcefully in the controversial document *Dominus Iesus,* which emphasised proclamation of Christ over dialogue.

Visiting India in 1999, the Pope delineated the Church's approach on the Asian continent, where he predicted "a great harvest of faith" in the years to come. He praised his hosts' non-Christian spiritual traditions but also preached the Gospel, and said the best way for Christians to evangelise was by living the Gospel values.

As the Pope aged, his rapport with young people remained consistently – and sometimes amazingly – fresh and energetic. World Youth Day celebrations seemed to bring out the Pope's good humour and vigour. He joked more easily with the young, and was happy in their company, but there was a serious side to all this, too.

Papal biographer Weigel, who attended many of the Youth Day celebrations and spoke extensively on Catholic college campuses, said it was striking how young people welcomed the Pope's challenge "not to settle for anything less than the religious and moral grandeur that they're capable of, under grace."

"He had a tremendous impact on the young, not by pandering to them, but by holding the bar of expectation high, all the time letting them know that he loves them and that Christ loves them."

As the years of this pontificate rolled by, the encyclicals and teaching documents became fewer and the speeches shorter. Those close to him said the Pope had clearly not run out of things to say, however – he was just saying them in different ways.

"At the start of the 21st century, the Pope continued to open people up to the transcendent, telling them that we're more than genetics, we're more than psychology, we're more than DNA," said Navarro-Valls, the Vatican spokesman.

The Pope also found time for more reflective writing, such as a small book of poetry - meditations that were inspired by the Sistine Chapel frescoes. He also wrote a book on his 20 years as a bishop in Poland. He authored a similar volume in 1996 on his life as a priest, an intensely personal review of the spiritual path that led to the papacy.

To discover how remarkable John Paul's papacy has been, one only has to look at its highlights:

• 1978, 16th October: Cardinal Karol Wojtyla of Krakow, Poland, is elected Pope. Taking the name John Paul II, he is the first non-Italian pope since 1523. At 58, he is the youngest since Pope Pius IX, who was elected at age 54. At the Mass formally inaugurating his ministry, he sets a theme for his pontificate with the words, "Be not afraid. Open wide the doors for Christ."

• 1979: Pope John Paul issues his first encyclical, on Christ, the Redeemer of mankind, and first major apostolic exhortation, on catechesis. He begins world travels with four trips: the Dominican Republic and Mexico; Poland; Ireland and the United States with a visit to the United Nations; and Turkey, where he and the patriarch of Constantinople inaugurate an official Catholic-Orthodox dialogue. Italian newspapers take to calling him "Cyclone Wojtyla." He convenes the first plenary session of cardinals in 400-plus years to discuss Vatican finances, curial structure and Church and culture.

• 1980: The pontiff calls Dutch bishops to Rome for a synod

to restore unity and discipline in the Dutch Church. He convenes a synod of the world's Ukrainian bishops. In a letter to the world's bishops, he warns against abuses in liturgy. He approves doctrinal congregation declaration condemning euthanasia. He declares St. Francis of Assisi patron saint of ecologists and St. Catherine of Siena a doctor of the Church. He travels to six African countries and to France, Brazil and West Germany. He presides over a world Synod of Bishops on the family and issues his second encyclical, on divine mercy.

• 1981: Pope John Paul supports workers' rights in a meeting with Lech Walesa and other leaders of Polish trade union Solidarity. He travels to Philippines, Guam and Japan with stopovers in Pakistan and Alaska. In three years he has matched the 15-year record of nine foreign trips by the "pilgrim Pope", Pope Paul VI. His beatification of 16 martyrs in Manila, Philippines, is the first beatification outside Rome since the 14th-century Avignon papacy. He is severely wounded and hospitalised for 11 weeks in an attempted assassination on May 13th. He issues his first social encyclical, on human work. He sends special delegations to world leaders with plea to reduce and eventually eliminate nuclear arms.

• 1982: John Paul makes a record seven trips abroad in one year, including successive visits to England and Argentina, then at war over the Falkland Islands. He canonises Polish World War II martyr St. Maximilian Kolbe. He makes Opus Dei the world's first personal prelature, a canonical jurisdiction headed by a bishop. He acknowledges need for public statements of Vatican finances.

• 1983: He promulgates a new Code of Canon Law, one of the major Church reform projects since the Second Vatican Council. He inaugurates a special holy year for the 1,950th anniversary of the Redemption. He issues a Charter of the Rights of the Family. He visits 12 countries in four foreign trips, starting with a marathon trip to seven Central American nations and Haiti. He presides over Synod of Bishops on theme of penance and reconciliation. His December visit to a Lutheran church in Rome marks the first time a Pope has preached in a Protestant church. He visits prison to meet Mehmet Ali Agca, his would-be assassin.

• 1984: Pope John Paul forms a new commission for authentic interpretation of Church laws, issues an apostolic letter on redemptive suffering and another on religious life. He visits 10 countries. In Korea he canonises 103 Korean martyrs. In Switzerland he calls the Church's ecumenical commitment irreversible during a visit to the World Council of Churches headquarters. He authorises bishops to allow Mass according to Tridentine rite under certain conditions. In five months of weekly audience talks on human love and sexuality, he reaffirms Church teaching against artificial contraception.

• 1985: In four trips abroad Pope John Paul visits 15 countries. He says belief in God and evolutionary theory can be compatible. New Vatican document says how Jews and Judaism should be presented in Catholic preaching and catechesis. New concordat with Italy replaces Lateran Treaty, updating Church-State relations in Italy. Pope issues encyclical on Sts. Cyril and Methodius, "Apostles of the Slavs." He calls widespread abortion in Europe "demographic suicide." He presides over extraordinary Synod of Bishops called to review state of Church

20 years after Vatican II. He convenes Council of Cardinals to discuss restructuring of Roman Curia.

• 1986: In four trips Pope John Paul visits nine countries; by end of year he has made 32 foreign trips in eight years as Pope. He caps a recent series of denunciations of the "inhumanity" of apartheid by calling South Africa's policy a "deplorable system." He breaks major new ground in Catholic relations with Jews and world religions, becoming first Pope since apostolic times to visit the Rome synagogue in April and convening a gathering of world religious leaders in October in Assisi to pray for peace. He warns theologians if they propagate dissent from Church moral teaching they violate the "fundamental right" of Catholics to learn Church doctrine. Doctrinal congregation instruction condemns homosexual activity. Pope issues his fifth encyclical, on the Holy Spirit. He forms a commission to write a universal Catholic catechism.

• 1987: Pope visits eight countries in four trips. He announces Marian Year starting in June and issues encyclical on Mary, Mother of the Redeemer. Vatican justice and peace office issues document on ethical issues of international debt. Doctrinal congregation issues instruction on procreation and beginning-of-life issues. Pope presides over world Synod of Bishops, on laity, setting the stage in preceding months with a series of talks on the role of the laity in the Church and world.

• 1988: He writes his second social encyclical, *On Social Concerns*. In an apostolic letter on women he defends women's equality but reaffirms that they cannot be ordained priests. He issues new legislation restructuring the Roman Curia. Among his four trips abroad, visiting 11 countries, is a trip to Strasbourg, France, to meet with the European Parliament, Council of Europe and European Human Rights Commission and Court.

• 1989: Pope John Paul issues an apostolic exhortation on the laity, reflecting the 1987 synod discussions. His four foreign trips take him to 13 countries. Responding to a public declaration by 163 European theologians accusing the Pope and Roman Curia of abusing their authority, the Pope says the Church cannot tolerate theological dissent that takes the form of a "parallel or alternative magisterium." The pontifical justice and peace council issues the first Vatican document devoted entirely to the issue of racism.

• 1990: Pope John Paul issues Code of Canons of the Eastern Churches, the first general codification of Church law for all Eastern-rite Catholics. He issues an apostolic constitution on Catholic higher education that sets worldwide norms for Catholic colleges and universities. He takes five trips abroad, visiting 12 countries. Vatican and Soviet Union establish diplomatic relations. Pope presides over Synod of Bishops on seminary formation and priestly life and ministry, reaffirms mandatory celibacy for priests.

• 1991: As Yugoslavia disintegrates, Pope John Paul speaks out repeatedly against civil warfare and ethnic cleansing in the Balkans. He tries in vain to prevent war in the Persian Gulf. He issues two encyclicals, one calling the Church to renew its missionary spirit, the other marking the 100th anniversary of papal social encyclicals with a commentary on the application of Catholic teaching to world political and economic systems. His world travels continue – to Portugal; Poland; Hungary; and Brazil.

• 1992: In three trips, Pope John Paul visits Dominican Republic and five African countries. He sends Cardinal Ratzinger to Czechoslovakia to regularise situation of married bishops and priests secretly ordained during years of Church persecution. He issues a pastoral instruction on social communications and an apostolic exhortation on priestly formation. In July he has a benign tumour removed from his colon and returns to work after his summer vacation. In June he approves, and in July formally issues, the first universal Catechism of the Catholic Church in more than 400 years.

• 1993: Pope John Paul convenes another interreligious meeting in Assisi to pray for peace. His five foreign trips in 1993 cover 11 countries, including the United States in August for World Youth Day in Denver. Responding to a flurry of reports of clergy sexual abuse of minors, the Pope addresses the issue several times and, in a letter to U.S. bishops, invokes Christ's words of woe to those who scandalise children. He issues *The Splendour of Truth,* the first papal encyclical ever on fundamentals of moral theology.

• 1994: Pope John Paul convenes in Rome the first-ever synod of African bishops, which denounces the hatred and lust for power tearing apart African societies. He establishes a Pontifical Academy for Life comprised of 70 scientists and scholars. In May he formally declares to world's bishops that the Church cannot ordain women and this teaching must be "definitively held" by Catholics. He leads global campaign to get U.N. Conference on Population and Development in Cairo to do more to promote marriage and family life and fight contraception and abortion. In October and in November visits Sicily, where he denounces Mafia. His November apostolic letter *Tertio Millennio Adveniente* sets agenda for Church reflection and renewal as it prepares for 2000.

• 1995: Pope John Paul removes French Bishop Jacques Gaillot from his diocese for opposing Church positions on issues like celibacy and women priests. Pope issues encyclical on the sacredness of all human life and one on ecumenism, in which he asks how a renewed papacy might serve as a ministry of unity for all Christians. He takes six trips abroad to 12 countries. In Africa he publishes an apostolic exhortation on the Church and social issues. As Fourth World Conference on Women approaches in Beijing, Pope John Paul writes letter to women apologising for past sexism in Church. Vatican supports most of the conference's final documents but takes strong exception to parts on women's health and rights. Amid Catholic signature campaigns in Europe urging married and women priests, doctrinal congregation strongly reaffirms Pope's 1994 statement against ordaining women.

• 1996: In yearly address to world's ambassadors to Vatican, Pope John Paul urges total ban on nuclear testing. In apostolic exhortation on consecrated life he calls for greater decision-making roles by women religious. He calls for global ban on land mines and decries global economic inequities that cause urban slum growth. In six trips he visits nine countries. In message to his Pontifical Academy of Sciences he calls evolution "more than a hypothesis," provoking new debates across Christian denominations. He meets with head of Anglican Communion, expressing commitment to ecumenism despite division over women's ordination. He marks his 50th year as a priest with a book, Gift and Mystery.

• 1997: Pope makes six trips to six nations. He names St. Therese of Lisieux a doctor of the Church. As key themes for the millennium he sets out evangelisation, Christian unity and restoration of justice, with a special focus on relief of Third World debt in the jubilee year. His support of debt relief helps spark wide religious backing for that effort. He takes more active stance in intervening against executions of criminals and a revision in the Catechism of the Catholic Church repudiates capital punishment in all but the most exceptional circumstances.

• 1998: In four trips, Pope John Paul visits four countries, including Cuba, where he confronts Fidel Castro on religious freedom. He writes an encyclical on faith and reason and an apostolic letter on the religious observance of Sunday. Devoting increasing attention to the coming millennium, he presides over two more regional synods of bishops – Asia in May and Oceania in December. In a papal bull declaring 2000 a holy year, he urges that it be marked by global action for justice as well as prayer and pilgrimages. He revises Canon Law to impose penalties on Catholics who persistently dissent from definitive Church teachings, and Vatican issues warnings or launches investigations against several theologians. New Vatican document acknowledges inadequacies in response of Church and individual Catholics to the Nazi Holocaust.

• 1999: Pope John Paul's visits to seven countries in five trips include a Mexico-U.S. visit to publish his apostolic exhortation, *The Church in America.* He warns against giving in to a culture of death and, in St. Louis, gains clemency for a man about to be executed. He also intercedes unsuccessfully for several other U.S. death-row inmates during the year. His 13-day visit to Poland is his seventh and longest since he became Pope. On his November trip to India he publishes *"The Church in Asia."* Now 79, he marks the U.N. Year of the Older Person with a pastoral reflection, *Letter to the Elderly.* On Christmas Eve he breaks open the Holy Door in St. Peter's, formally opening the Great Jubilee of the Year 2000.

• 2000: In a year filled with public appearances for jubilee events, three stand out: his visit in March to Jerusalem, where millions are moved by his prayer at the Western Wall; his prayer service on the Day of Forgiveness, asking forgiveness of all those harmed in the name of the Church; and his celebration of Mass for two million people gathered in Rome for World Youth Day. He travels to Fatima, Portugal, to beatify Francisco and Jacinta Marta, two of the three children who saw visions of Mary there in 1917. At the end of the beatification Mass, the Vatican releases the third secret of Fatima, a vision of the gunning down of a "bishop clothed in white." He condemns Dutch legislation allowing homosexuals to marry and calls the holding of World Gay Pride 2000 in Rome an affront to the Church and jubilee year. He also condemns British decision to allow destruction of human embryos for stem cell use.

• 2001: Pope John Paul issues apostolic letter on the new millennium, formally closing jubilee year 2000 and setting out a vision for the Church's future. In Kazakstan, two weeks after the 9/11 terrorist attacks, he warns that "religions must never be used as a reason for conflict."

• 2002: Pope convenes world religion leaders again for peace prayers in Assisi. In three trips abroad he visits six countries,

including an eighth visit to his native Poland and a trip to Canada for World Youth Day. As U.S. crisis of clergy sexual abuse of minors burgeons, he calls an emergency meeting of U.S. cardinals in April to decide how to respond. He declares that no one who would harm children has a place in the priesthood or religious life. He declares a year of the Rosary and proclaims five "Luminous Mysteries" of the Rosary, adding to the traditional trio of Joyful, Sorrowful and Glorious mysteries. Vatican excommunicates seven women who refuse to renounce their priestly ordinations by a former Catholic priest illegally ordained a bishop. Pope canonises St. Josemaria Escriva de Balaguer, founder of Opus Dei. He approves new Church laws to remove sexually abusive priests from ministry and from priesthood if warranted.

• 2003: Papal travels to Croatia and Bosnia-Herzegovina in June extending the record of his foreign trips to 101 within his first 25 years as Pope. Also on the 2003 list was a September trip to Slovakia. Vatican becomes a hub of global diplomatic activity as the Pope leads efforts to stave off war in Iraq. He initiates creation of short version of catechism. He pushes repeatedly for reference to Europe's Christian roots in new constitution of the European Union. He issues an encyclical on the Eucharist in the life of the Church. He approves Vatican document that calls same-sex unions harmful to society and says Catholic lawmakers are obliged to oppose their legalisation. He schedules the beatification of Mother Teresa of Calcutta for the 19th of October, just three days after the official 25th anniversary of his election as Pope.

• 2004: On the occasion of the 150th anniversary of the promulgation of the Dogma of the Immaculate Conception, the Pope memorably joins other August pilgrims seeking healing at Lourdes. He also visits Switzerland to coincide with the National Meeting of Young Catholics of Switzerland. He receives in audience His Holiness Bartholomew I, ecumenical patriarch of Constantinople, and they sign a joint declaration of understanding. This is followed later in the year by the delivery of the relics of Sts. John Chrysostom and Gregory Nazianzen, Bishops and Doctors of the Church, to Bartholomew I. He offers a gift of the Icon of Kazan Mother of God to the Russian Orthodox Church and the Russian people. The Apostolic Letter entitled *Mane nobiscum Domine* announces the Year of the Eucharist in October.

• 2005: Pope John Paul publishes a 22-page book entitled Memory and Identity, a transcript of a series of conversations between the Pope and a group of friends in the garden of the Papal Summer Residence at Castelgandolfo during the Summer of 1993.

A young Karol Jozef Wojtyla, the future Pope John Paul II, is pictured with his father, also Karol, in a photo taken in the mid-1920s. Wife and mother Emilia died when Karol was nine. His older brother, Edmund, died of scarlet fever three years after their mother's death.

An infant Karol Wojtyla is pictured in an undated photo in Wadowice, Poland. The future Pope John Paul II was born 18th May, 1920, the second son of Karol and Emilia Wojtyla. His older brother, Edmund, was born in 1906.

Early Years

Infant Karol Wojtyla is held by his mother, Emilia, in this undated photo. Emilia died in 1929.

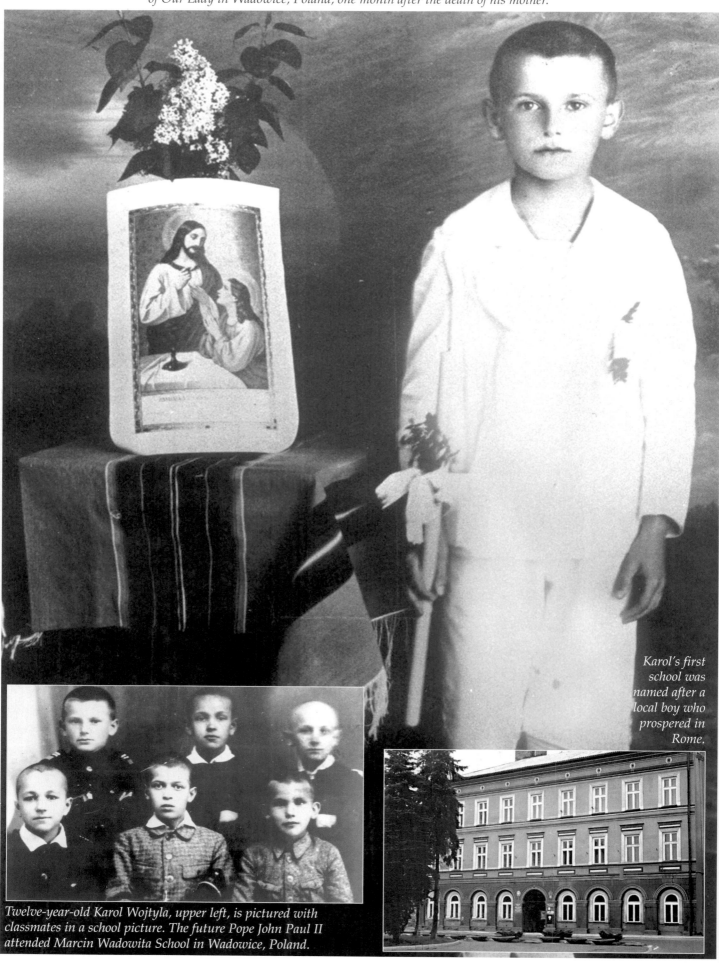

Karol Wojtyla is pictured at his First Communion on 25th May, 1929. The future Pope John Paul II received the sacrament at the Church of Our Lady in Wadowice, Poland, one month after the death of his mother.

Karol's first school was named after a local boy who prospered in Rome.

Twelve-year-old Karol Wojtyla, upper left, is pictured with classmates in a school picture. The future Pope John Paul II attended Marcin Wadowita School in Wadowice, Poland.

Wojtyla recieves his first two minor orders

Krakow, 17th December, 1944

After two years as a seminarian, Karol Wojtyla, aged 24, received the first two minor orders. He was also tonsured, according to the medieval rite. Accession to the priesthood entails a long apprenticeship. The code of Canon Law states that all four minor orders cannot be conferred on the same day (The four degrees of minor order are porter, exorcist, lector, and acolyte). Once one reaches the sub-diaconate, the first of the three major orders, "clerics are compelled to the recital of the breviary." Next is the diaconate, nomination as a deacon, and then the ministry, itself subdivided into the priesthood and the episcopate. Archbishops and Cardinals are dignitaries. To complete his training, Mgr. Sapieha sent Karol to spend a few weeks in Raciborowice, a parish a few miles northeast of Krakow. The seminarians so rarely got out of the Archbishop's Palace, for fear of German raids, that Karol treated this sojourn as a "holiday." This in no way prevented him from feeling extremely grateful towards Fr. Jozef Jamroz, the parish priest, and the assistant priests, including Frs. Franciszek Szymonek and Adam Biela, a native of Wadowice, from whom he learned a lot.

A 1946 photo of Fr. Karol Wojtyla shows him as a newly ordained priest. The future Pope John Paul II received the Sacrament of Holy Orders on 1st November, 1946, and celebrated his first Mass as a priest in the crypt of St. Leonard at Wawel Cathedral in Krakow, Poland.

A group of children pose with a young Father Karol Wojtyla during his time as assistant pastor of a rural parish in Niegowic.

Father Karol Wojtyla

Krakow, 1st November, 1946

"You must first finish that which has been commenced." These were the words of Mgr. Sapieha, archbishop of Krakow, to Karol Wojtyla when the young seminarian asked permission to train to become a monk. After four years, his time in the seminary was nearing an end, as he had just been ordained a priest.

The ceremony took place in the private chapel of the Archbishop's Palace. Karol received the blessing of Mgr. Sapieha, alone, after six days of spiritual retreat. The dank grey day outside contrasted strongly with the joy and light which filled his whole being. At the very moment when, at long last, he received the laying on of hands, a strong memory came to mind. It was the image of Jetzy Zachuta, a young man who, like him, had pursued his studies at the seminary clandestinely, under the Occupation, and who one day disappeared. It was upon reading the list of names of Poles arrested by the Germans, the following day, that he learned of his friend's fate. He had fallen into enemy hands and was due to be executed. It was towards him, for him, that Karol Wojtyla said his first prayer as a priest, on the feast of All Saints, which the Church normally takes to be a day of happiness.

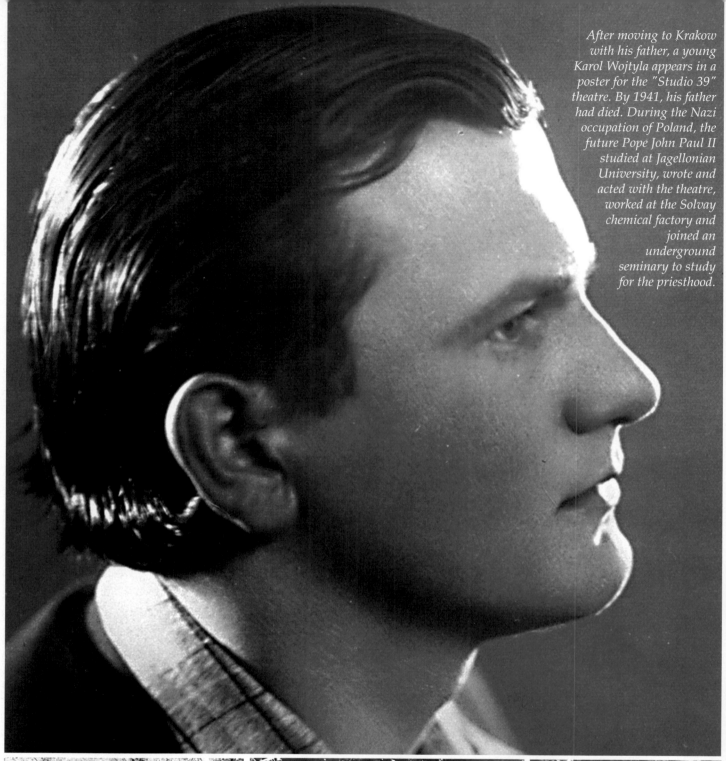

After moving to Krakow with his father, a young Karol Wojtyla appears in a poster for the "Studio 39" theatre. By 1941, his father had died. During the Nazi occupation of Poland, the future Pope John Paul II studied at Jagellonian University, wrote and acted with the theatre, worked at the Solvay chemical factory and joined an underground seminary to study for the priesthood.

Fr. Karol Wojtyla is pictured on a cycling outing in Poland in the early 1950s. His strong interest in outdoor activities continued through his years as Pope John Paul II, until the effects of age kept him away from strenuous pursuits.

Fr. Karol Wojtyla is pictured reading in a kayak in 1955. Three years later during a kayaking trip, he was called to Warsaw for the announcement that he was to become a bishop.

Bishop Karol Wojtyla lathers up for an outdoor shave during a 1959 mountain-climbing expedition. Pope John Paul II maintained an active outdoor life throughout his tenure as bishop, cardinal and Pope.

Bishop Karol Wojtyla concentrates during an event at Lublin Catholic University in Poland. In the mid-1950s, the future Pope served as chair of ethics at the university, the only Catholic university allowed to operate during communist rule of the Eastern bloc.

As bishop of Krakow in the 1960s, Karol Wojtyla was a prolific writer. In one of his books about his time as a bishop, the pontiff described his confrontations with Poland's Communist government and his efforts to create a new style of ministry.

His motto: *Totus tuus*

Krakow, October 1958

Like every other new bishop, Karol Wojtyla had to choose a motto. He took his, *Totus tuus* ('All for you'), from a 17th century French saint, Louis-Marie Grignion de Montfort, whose work had greatly impressed him. It had taught him that popular piety, devotion to the Virgin and mystical spirituality all go together.

Bishop Karol Wojtyla prays following his episcopal ordination in September 1958.

Raised to cardinal in Sistine Chapel

Vatican, 28th June, 1967

The archbishop of Krakow was one of 27 cardinals named by Paul VI. For Karol Wojtyla, it was undoubtedly recompense for his intense pastoral activity in Poland, which had proved him to be one of the most effective executors of the Council's decisions. That afternoon, all the new cardinals were given their red birettas by the Pope. They donned their cardinal's vestments in the sacristy (Sala dei Paramenti) and, led by the doyen of the Sacred College, they processed into the Sistine Chapel. There, seated in front of them, the Pope pronounced the sacred words: "For the glory of the all-powerful God and for the glory of the Church, accept this sign of the dignity of cardinal through which you will become the defender of the Faith and pledge your blood." In accordance with ancient tradition, each cardinal was assigned a church in Rome by Pope Paul VI. Karol Wojtyla was given San Cesareo, a beautiful building near the baths of Caracalla. Mgr. Wojtyla owed his rapid rise to the position of cardinal to the vigour of his evangelical message, which is crystal clear, straightforward and extremely precise.

A vibrant Cardinal Karol Wojtyla is pictured in this undated photo. As the Archbishop of Krakow, he oversaw more than 300 parishes with 1,000 priests, began construction of a new church and promoted dialogue with the Jewish community in Krakow.

Cardinal Karol Wojtyla of Krakow celebrates his 50th birthday in Wadowice, Poland, 18th May, 1970. During the celebrations, the future Pope John Paul II consecrated the new bells of his hometown Church of Our Lady.

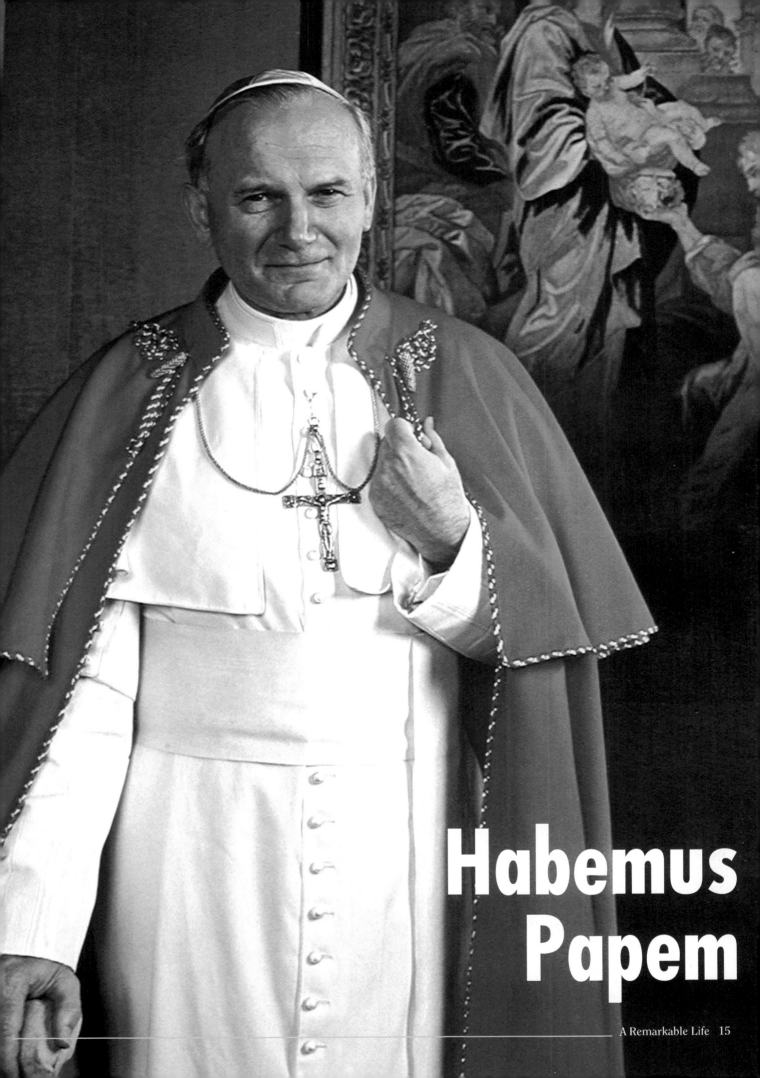

Habemus Papem

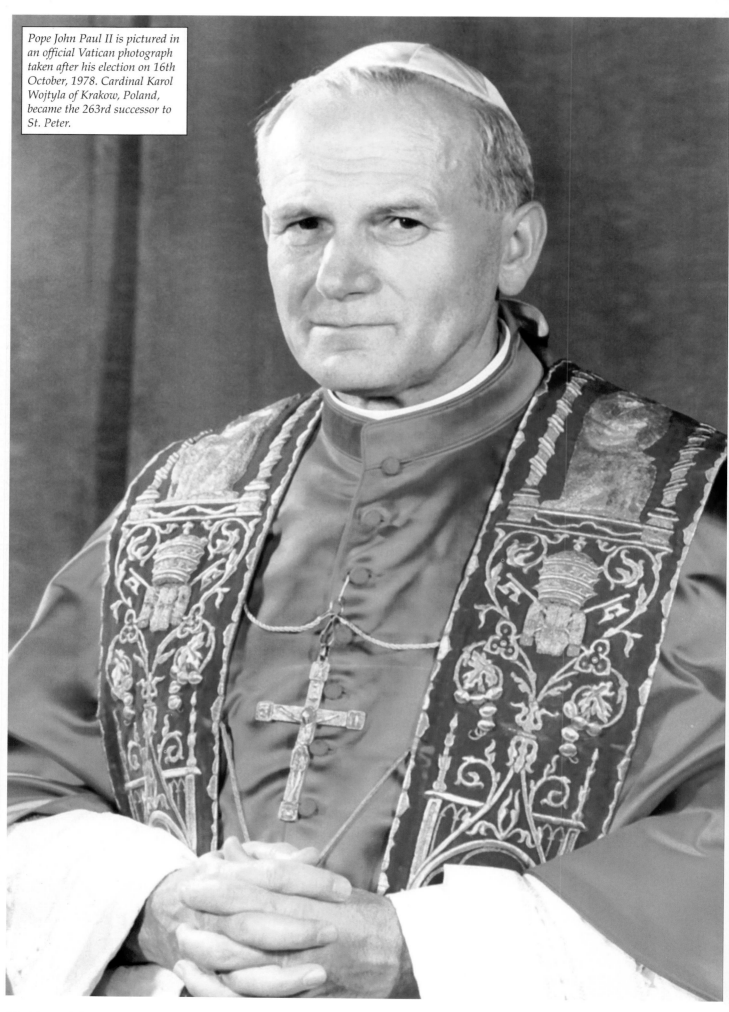

Pope John Paul II is pictured in an official Vatican photograph taken after his election on 16th October, 1978. Cardinal Karol Wojtyla of Krakow, Poland, became the 263rd successor to St. Peter.

For the past two conclaves, the prelates who burn all the papers and documents used for the election, and who have to stoke the stove from which the white smoke issues if a pope has been elected (or black if not), have used a smoke-producing device in the Vatican chimney, in order to avoid even the slightest ambiguity.

The world could not believe its eyes: the man who waved to them from his new home in St. Peter's Basilica was Polish.

Worldwide reaction

The news spread quickly to the furthest corners of the country.

On the feast of St. Hedwig, a patron saint of Poland, the 111 Cardinals of the conclave chose Karol Wojtyla of Krakow, at the eighth ballot, to follow in Peter's footsteps. The first non-Italian for 455 years, he was the first Polish Pope and, at 58, the youngest since Pius IX.

The announcement, coming an hour after the white smoke had appeared from the chimney above the Sistine Chapel, stunned the huge crowd waiting in St. Peter's Square and the world at large; it appeared to be a thrilling redemption of a period of sadness, uncertainty and anxiety.

His election delighted 'conservatives' and 'progressives' alike. He was reported to be both a rigidly conservative theologian as well as a pastor who had worked side by side with factory men and women.

And his age finally disposed of the notion that popes should be very old men and excited those looking forward to a long and fruitful reign, paving the way into the next millennium.

After the initial shock, there came euphoric jubilation as church and secular leaders from around the world expressed their admiration for the Cardinals' bold new step, as for the second time in two months, the conclave had ignored safety and instead voted with courage and imagination.

Naturally, the election of the first Polish Pope was greeted with particular delight by Poles around the world. In Britain, many spontaneous special services of celebration were held, including one at Ealing Abbey in London where Fr. Ladislaus Honkisz, a personal friend of the new Pope, told a congregation of 400, many in national costume, that the election was "our joy and our great duty".

Mgr. Karol Zielinski, the Polish Vicar Delegate and National Director of the 120 Polish priests serving in this country said: "We are very happy. It is a surprise for us but we are enjoying it."

Tadeusz Wirth, a spokesman for the Polish Association of the Sovereign Military Order of Malta, said: "We are happy, no doubt about it. He is young, that is very important, and very well educated."

Ladislaw Balon, who went to school with the Pope at Wadowice, not far from Krakow, said: "He is a courageous man. I remember that his father used to sit him up on the railings of the altar. At school he was always brilliant and went to the top of the class."

In Poland itself, the news of Cardinal Wojtyla's election was greeted with disbelief followed by amazement and rejoicing. Polish Radio announced the news as the lead item in its 7pm news bulletin and the official news agency, P.A.P., carried the story a few minutes later.

Warsaw, which had been basking in sunshine all day, suddenly erupted with joy. Catholics and non-Catholics took to the streets and filled the churches. Special Masses were said at Warsaw's huge cathedral of St. John, and St. Mary's Cathedral, Krakow.

A Polish Government spokesman said: "This election has a special significance – it is the first time the Pope has been a Pole, a member of a nation which went through the war and accomplished profound transformation and is advancing along the road of all-round development.

"The Poles attach special value to everything that serves peace and encourages peaceful co-operation of nations. Therefore, we received with attention the fact that the new Pope chose the name John Paul II, the name of his great predecessor."

Pope still dazed over own election

Rome, 17th October, 1978
One of John Paul II's first visits was to the bedside of his old Polish friend, Mgr. Andrzej Deskur, still suffering from his recent heart attack. The Holy Father was not able to talk to the man who had initiated him into the esoteric ways of the Vatican because he was still unconscious. Having come to the clinic without any security guards, he had to be reminded, at the end of his visit, that he should bless all those present. At the top of his voice and smiling, he said to the nurses: "It's not finished, I've got to bless you ... They are teaching me how to behave like a pope!"

The election of John Paul II dominated the news in October, 1978. Most secular newspaper headlines emphasised that the new pontiff was from behind the 'Iron Curtain' and that he signalled a huge break in tradition for the Catholic Church:

The Times: "Polish Cardinal becomes Pope John Paul II: First non-Italian for 450 years: a surprise choice."

The Guardian: "Cardinals turn to Poland for new Pope."

Daily Express: "Iron Curtain Pope: It's John Paul as the Cardinals choose a worker's son from Poland."

Daily Mail: "The Iron Curtain Pope – an astonishing break with centuries of Italian tradition. A Pope to put the fear of God in the persecutors."

The Sun: "He's John Paul II – The Iron Curtain Pope. The man who is not afraid to speak out for freedom."

Inside, the lead writers paid tribute both to the man and the Cardinals who had elected him.

The Times called the election "an event of extreme importance. As a Pole, Pope John Paul II has a very great particular experience of some of the greatest problems that confront the Church."

Of the Cardinals, it said: "They have elected a Pope to face the problem of Communism: there is no country which has a deeper experience of Communism, or more skill in handling Communist power, than Poland.

"They have started the Church on a journey the end of which cannot be known."

Words – response

Cardinal Basil Hume, a member of the Conclave and often mentioned as a possible outsider himself, said: "I am delighted with the election of Cardinal Karol Wojtyla. My knowledge of him leads me to hope that he will prove to be an outstanding Pope. He is likely to be a profound teacher, a fearless leader and a courageous witness for justice and Christian love."

Archbishop Thomas Winning of Glasgow: "The bishops, clergy and people of the Archdiocese of Glasgow offer affectionate and prayerful greetings and congratulations to your Holiness on your election to the See of Peter, pledge anew their loyalty to the Vicar of Christ and assure you of our constant prayers that the Holy Spirit will guide and sustain you during a long and fruitful pontificate."

Archbishop Thomas O Fiaich of Armagh: "From a country which, like Poland, is far away from Rome, we give thanks to the Lord for the gift of the new Holy Father to lead us in the communion of saints and Christian love. In pledging our loyalty and affection to him, we pray that God will bless his pontificate and that Our Lady, whose aid he invoked so affectionately when giving his first blessing, will always be his support."

Archbishop George Dwyer, the then president of the Bishops' Conference of England and Wales, said: "The choice of Cardinal Wojtyla is refreshing and exhilarating. As a Polish bishop he has had to face every day the problem of how to live a Christian life in an atheist state. Those who are trying to do so will take new heart as this election shows them that the Church not only remembers them but regards them as its leaders. The Cardinals have taken a man from the front line and made him Commander-in-Chief. Catholics everywhere will be delighted to have this sign of confidence in the Church. The wisdom and courage of the Cardinals in making this choice are a tribute to the great Paul VI who appointed nearly all of them."

Archbishop Derek Worlock of Liverpool, who had worked with Cardinal Wojtyla on the Council of Laity for the previous ten years and described him as "a great friend", said: "I am overjoyed at the news of Cardinal Wojtyla's election as Pope. It is an immensely courageous decision by the Cardinals but they have placed their faith in a man of deep personal courage and proven ability. All who know him will testify to the brilliance of his intellect. He is a man who listens well, studies all views carefully and then produces a careful and brilliant opinion or decision which he presents humbly and defends courageously. He is a man of peace and a defender of principles and rights. He is a man who has known suffering and hardship so that the joy of his presence is the more compelling."

Bishop Hugh Lindsay, the chairman of the Catholic Information Service in England and Wales in 1978, said: "The new Pope is another pleasant surprise. He is all we had hoped for, a man of deep well-tested faith, a younger man and a warm pastoral bishop. When you find that he is also a good theologian and that he speaks Italian well enough to charm a Roman crowd, you are beginning to understand our joy at his election."

Dr. Donald Coggan, Archbishop of Canterbury: "I am delighted to hear the news. We send him every good wish. He will be in our prayers and in the prayers of the world-wide Anglican Communion."

Prime Minister, James Callaghan: "I offer to your Holiness on the assumption of your high office my greetings and my very best wishes for the success of your pontificate."

Pope's role in the collapse of Communism

Hundreds of thousands of Polish citizens line the streets of Warsaw near Victory Square in June 1979 as Pope John Paul II's motorcade drives past. Poles were ecstatic at the first visit of their beloved Karol Wojtyla as pontiff, in contrast to the no doubt uneasy Communist puppet-government.

Cardinal Karol Wojtyla (left) confers with Cardinal Stefan Wyszynski, Polish primate, in this undated photo. Cardinal Wyszynski opposed both the German and Russian occupations of Poland and was imprisoned as a threat to the Communist regime in the 1950s. More than a generation later, Pope John Paul II supported Solidarity, the workers' movement in Poland that eventually threw off Communist rule.

Cardinal Karol Wojtyla celebrates a dedication Mass at Mother of God, Queen of Poland Church in Nowa Huta, Poland, 15th May, 1977. The completion of the church was a landmark for the future Pope John Paul II, who fought for a new church in this modern, Communist-worker town for more than 10 years. The parish numbered some 20,000 members and the cardinal often compared the poor parish in Nowa Huta to the humble Nativity grotto in Bethlehem.

President Ronald W. Reagan reaches out to Pope John Paul II at the Pope's arrival in Miami in September, 1987, for a U.S. visit. Pope John Paul paid tribute to Reagan on his death, noting his important role in the fall of European communism. The two men are often credited as the key figures in bringing about the collapse of Communism.

At the monastery of Jasna Gora in Czestochowa, Poland, Pope John Paul II greets throngs of Poles waiting for a glimpse of their native son during the first trip to his homeland in June, 1979. The pontiff's visit motivated workers to form Solidarity, the first independent trade union in a Communist-ruled country.

Pope John Paul II celebrates Mass at Victory Square in Warsaw during his first trip to Poland as Pope in June, 1979. Travels throughout the country took him to Krakow, the shrine of Jasna Gora at Czestochowa and the Auschwitz concentration camp, among other places. More than 12 million of his countrymen attended his Masses and speeches over the eight-day visit, much to the consternation of the Communist authorities.

Crowds cheer in the streets of Warsaw, Poland, on 4th June, 1979, waiting for the arrival of Pope John Paul II on his first visit to Poland as Pope. The pontiff's first and subsequent visits gave energy to the Polish people and helped the Solidarity movement to eventually topple Communism in Poland.

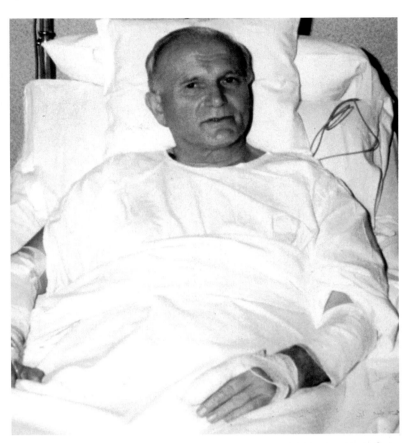

Pope John Paul II lies injured in his jeep after being shot by Turkish gunman Mehmet Ali Agca on 13th May, 1981, in St. Peter's Square. Italy granted Agca clemency after he had served 19 years for the assassination attempt.

Pope John Paul II is pictured at Rome's Gemelli hospital following his injuries from an assassination attempt on 13th May, 1981. It is strongly suspected that the gunman was working under orders from the Soviet authorities.

Former Polish President and Solidarity founder Lech Walesa stands at the front gate of the Gdansk shipyard on 29th August, 2000. The trade union, which sparked an anti-Communist movement in Poland in the 1980s, celebrated its 20th anniversary that year. Walesa and the Pope worked together as a pivotal pairing in the fall of Polish Communism.

Pope John Paul II waves to Polish pilgrims as he arrives at the Sanctuary of Divine Mercy in the Lagiewniki suburb of Krakow, Poland, 17th August, 2002. The four-day visit to Poland was the Pope's ninth to his homeland.

A crowd estimated at 2.2 million greets Pope John Paul II at a Mass in Blonia Park, Krakow, Poland on 18th August, 2002. Local Church officials said it was the largest crowd ever to attend a papal liturgy in Poland. It demonstrated the love of the Polish people towards the country's favourite son, recognising his prominant role in the history of their counntry. (CNS)

Other former-Eastern Bloc countries also recognised the huge role played by the Pope in the collapse of Communism. Here, Pope John Paul II prays at the Hill of Crosses in Siauliai, Lithuania, in September, 1993. Some 200,000 crosses, statues and rosaries were placed on the hill in defiance of former Communist leaders. A year after his visit there, the Pope donated a large crucifix for the hill.

Ireland visit

The Pope arrives at Dublin Airport.

Day by day with the Pope

Saturday 29th September, 1979

10.00: The Pope arrives at Dublin Airport in the Aer Lingus flagship. Almost his first words are of peace: "Peace to all of you who are in Christ." The Pope is welcomed by President Hillery, members of the Government and by all the Irish bishops.

10.40: The Pope leaves by helicopter for the Papal nunciature in Nivan Road, Cabra.

11.30: The Pope leaves by helicopter for Phoenix Park, where 1.3 million people – the largest single gathering in Ireland's history – are present at Mass beneath the 120-foot-high steel cross.

12.00: The Mass begins. In his homily, the Pope speaks of the unshakeable faith of the Irish down the ages and of their great missionary work. He stresses the importance of our union with Christ in the Eucharist which must be expressed in our behaviour.

14.00: The Pope begins his drive through the cheering millions in Phoenix Park in the 'Popemobile'. Pathways through the 'pens' enable everyone to get within a few yards of him.

15.30: The Pope leaves by helicopter for Drogheda.

16.00: The Pope presides at a Liturgy of the Word before another huge crowd, many from the North. He venerates the relics of St. Oliver Plunkett, martyred Archbishop of Armagh. Here he makes the most impassioned plea for peace. He says to the men of violence: "On my knees, I beg you to turn away from the paths of violence and to return to the paths of peace."

17.30: The Pope returns by helicopter to Dublin Airport.

18.00: The triumphal motorcade through Dublin begins. At Aras an Uachtarain he meets President Hillery.

19.00: The Pope returns by car to the nunciature, where he meets the Prime Minister, Mr. Jack Lynch, the Government and Diplomatic Corps.

21.00: The Pope meets other representatives of other Christian Churches in the Dominican Convent, Cabra. His plea: all Christians must unite against violence.

21.15: The Pope meets journalists covering the visit in St. Patrick's Hall, Dominican Convent, Cabra.

Sunday 30th September, 1979

8.00: The Pope meets a group of mentally-handicapped people at the Dominican Convent, Cabra.

8.30: He meets members of the Polish community at the nunciature.

9.00: The Pope leaves by helicopter for Galway.

10.00: The Pope arrives in Galway, where a quarter of a million young people give him a rapturous welcome. During Mass his homily is interrupted for more than 10 minutes by a cheering, flag- and banner-waving demonstration of affection and loyalty. The Pope tells the young people gathered: "I believe in the youth of Ireland."

12.30: The drive through the crowd begins.

The Popemobile ziz-zags through the thousands who turned out to see the Pontiff in Dublin's Phoenix Park. In order to get a better view, many climbed a pylon.

1.00: Lunch in Galway.

14.10: The papal helicopter leaves Galway.

14.30: The Pope arrives at Knock.

15.00: Open-air Mass celebrates the centenary of the vision of Our Lady, St. Joseph and St. John.

17.00: The Pope prays at the scene of the vision, the gable-end of the old church.

17.10: Papal drive through the crowd is scheduled. Mist at Dublin Airport compels him to leave, cutting short the drive. In the evening the Pope has a formal meeting with the Irish bishops at the Dominican Convent, Cabra.

Monday 1st October, 1979

7.30: The Pope leaves the nunciature by helicopter for Maynooth, where he meets students for the priesthood, clerics and local people.

8.00: In the Maynooth College chapel he speaks to seminarians, then addresses the crowd. He tells the seminarians that the 1980s could be a decisive period for the Faith in Ireland. He urges priests and religious not to take God off the streets by wearing secular dress.

9.00: The Pope leaves for Limerick.

10.15: Mass begins on Limerick racecourse. The Pope emphasises the sanctity of human life from conception to death and the sanctity and indissolubility of marriage.

12.00: The Pope drives through the crowds.

12.30: The papal helicopter departs for Shannon Airport.

12.50: Arrival at Shannon and the official farewell from President Hillery and Cardinal O Fiaich. There is a guard of honour and a military band.

13.30: The Aer Lingus flagship St. Patrick, takes off for Boston, USA, and another ecstatic welcome for Pope John Paul II.

Unity Vigil

The Pope wanted to make an unscheduled visit to a vigil for reconciliation and peace held in Dublin at the end of his first day in Ireland.

Unfortunately, with his tight schedule running nearly two hours late by the end of the day, this became impossible.

Cardinal Willebrands, President of the Secretariat for Promoting Christian Unity, was among those present in St. Patrick's Protestant cathedral. The President of the Irish Republic, Dr. Patrick Hillery, and the Irish Prime Minister, Mr. Jack Lynch, came direct from their meetings with the Pope to join the congregation of over 2,000 who packed every corner of the cathedral.

The vigil, introduced by Fr. Michael Hurley SJ, director of the Irish School of Ecumenics, included prayers, readings and religious drama.

The vigil took as its themes: youth; people at work; Ireland North and South; the deprived. Cardinal O Fiaich described the vigil as a wonderful initiative and an important milestone in the work of ecumenism in Ireland.

The Cardinal wished every blessing on the gathering, which, he hoped, would be an instrument of reconciliation and hope.

Reconciliation

A report on the Pope's ecumenical encounter with leaders of the Christian Churches in Ireland.

The Pope told representatives of other Christian Churches in Ireland, "Let no one ever doubt the commitment of the Catholic Church to the pursuit of the unity of Christians."

His meeting, nearly two hours behind schedule, took place on the first day of his visit to Ireland, at the Dominican Convent, Cabra.

He said: "The work of reconciliation, the road to unity, may be long and difficult. All Christians in Ireland must join together in opposing all violence and all assaults against the human

(above) The Pope waves to the Phoenix Park crowd.
(below) The moment of the consecration at Phoenix Park.

person – from whatever quarter they come – and in finding the Christian answer to the grave problems of Northern Ireland.

"We must all be ministers of reconciliation. We must by example as well as by word try to move citizens, communities and politicians towards the ways of tolerance, co-operation and love.

"No fear of criticism, no risk of resentment, must deter us from this task."

All the Church of Ireland bishops were present at the meeting, led by the Most Rev. George O'Simms, Archbishop of Armagh and Primate of All Ireland, and the Most Rev. Henry McAdoo, Archbishop of Dublin.

They said before the meeting that it was their earnest prayer that the visit of the Pope would bring improved relationships between the Churches and advance peace and reconciliation in Ireland.

The Presbyterian representatives were led by the Very Rev. Dr. A. J. Weir, Clerk of the General Assembly. However, the moderator, the Rev. William Craig, was not present. He said it would be inappropriate for him to meet the Pope.

The Presbyterians told the Pope that the ecumenical scene was at a standstill, if not in retreat. They referred to the tragic situation in Ireland, where communities as well as Churches were seen to be divided or even in confrontation.

They said: "Many feel threatened by the activities of the Roman Catholic Church".

The Rev. Vincent Parkin, President of the Methodist Church in Ireland, led the six members of his Church. Also present was Canon William Arlow of St. Anne's Cathedral in Belfast. A former secretary of the Irish Council of Churches, Canon Arlow had special responsibility for ecumenical affairs. He was a guest of Cardinal O Fiaich in Rome when the Cardinal received his red hat on 30th June [1979]. The Chief Rabbi of Ireland, Dr. Isaac Cohen, was also at the short meeting with the Pope.

Earlier in the day, the Pope had said in Drogheda: "May no Irish Protestant think that the Pope is an enemy, a danger or a threat."

The Pope said that his desire was that Protestants would see in him "a friend and brother in Christ".

'I Love Youth'

The youth of Ireland gave the Pope a tumultuous welcome when he offered Mass for them in Galway on the second day of his visit to Ireland.

"I believe in the youth of Ireland," the Pope told over 250,000 young people between the ages of 16 and 24, who represented every parish in Ireland. They cheered him for over ten minutes.

"When I look to you, I see the Ireland of the future. Tomorrow you will have the power to make dreams come true. Tomorrow Ireland will depend on you."

The response to the Pope's sermon was overwhelming. The young people cheered him and sang time and again: "He's got the whole world in his hands".

The Pope was visibly moved by the spontaneous display of affection by the young people in the crowd, estimated at about 400,000.

In contrast to the warm sunshine of the day before in Dublin, Galway was cold and wet. However, this did nothing to dampen the spirits of the young people, who waved banners and sang many songs for the Pope, including "The Rivers of Babylon".

In his sermon, the Pope referred to "the painful events that for over ten years have been taking place in Northern Ireland."

The thousands of young people who came from the north knew only too well what the Pope meant. Some had themselves been

An emotion-filled youth steps up on to the podium during the Pope's celebration of a youth Mass at the Ballybrit Racecourse, Galway.

caught by the violence: Damian Irwin, from Belfast, who assisted the Pope during the Mass, was maimed in a bomb blast two years earlier and now walks with the aid of an artificial leg.

Richard Moore, also 19, from the Creggan in Derry, was blinded by a rubber bullet. He was presented to the Pope during the Offertory procession.

The Pope, who had a remarkable rapport with young people, was in no hurry to leave after his long drive round the Ballybrit racecourse, though his schedule was well behind time.

With the Sick at Mary's Hill

And so to Knock – the village at the heart of the Papal visit.

When the red helicopter carrying the Pope came into view on the Sunday afternoon, it was a dream come true for Mgr. Horan, the parish priest who had suggested the Pope's visit in the year celebrating the centenary of the apparition at Knock.

In the morning, Mgr. Horan was walking quietly round the grounds as a light rain fell and 400,000 pilgrims gathered under grey skies.

Looking relaxed and the picture of contentment, he told me: "I feel very excited, I am not an excitable person. I am very pragmatic. But I am looking forward to the moment when the helicopter lands."

With Archbishop Cunnane of Tuam, in whose diocese Knock is situated, he welcomed the successor of Peter to Cnoc Mhuire – Mary's Hill – as Knock is known in Gaelic.

As the helicopter circled the crowd, they forgot the cold, the wind and the showers of rain and cheered the Holy Father. Those among the crowd who had braved the icy wind on the hill beside the Basilica of Our Lady, Queen of Ireland, had the first glimpse of him as he stepped out of the helicopter and moved up a ramp to the ambulatory. Wave after wave of cheering greeted his appearance.

He went into the Basilica, where 3,000 sick pilgrims were waiting, and told them: "The Gospels are filled with instances where Our Lord shows His particular love and concern for the sick and all those in pain. Jesus loved those who suffered and this attitude has been passed on to His Church.

"Today I am happy to be with the sick and the handicapped. I have come to give witness to Christ's love for you and to tell you that the Church and the Pope love you too. They revere and

Pope John Paul II blesses a young girl during his visit to Knock Shrine.

esteem you. They are convinced that there is something very special about your mission in the Church."

The Pope said that Christ called upon the sick and everyone who suffered to collaborate with Him in the salvation of the world. Jesus had made it clear that the value of suffering was linked to His own suffering and death.

The sick and suffering were called by Christ to love with a special intensity. They were to remember that Our Lady was close to them: "She will never leave you all alone."

He told the handmaids and helpers that they were performing "not only a work of charity, but also a task of evangelisation."

The Holy Father then went to the outdoor altar to offer Mass with 200 concelebrants, including cardinals and bishops from several countries, 26 priests representing the 26 dioceses of Ireland, 37 representing the Congregation of Major Religious Superiors and the missionary societies, and more than a dozen priests born in Knock.

Distinguished guests included President Hillery of Ireland.

The Pope said: "Here I am at the goal of my journey to Ireland: the Shrine of Our Lady of Knock."

He came because he wanted all of them to know that his devotion to Mary united him in a very special way with the people of Ireland, who had a long tradition of devotion to Our Lady.

"For a whole century now, you have sanctified this place of pilgrimage through your prayers, through your sacrifices, through your penance. All those who have come here have received blessings through the intervention of Mary."

He said it was an important time in the history of the Universal Church and in particular the Church in Ireland.

"So many things have changed, so many valuable new insights have been gained into what it means to be Christian.

"So many new problems have to be faced by the faithful, either because of the increased pace of change in society, or because of the new demands that are made on the people of God – demands to live to the fullest the mission of evangelisation."

Every generation was like a new continent to be won for Christ.

"The Church must constantly look for new ways that will enable her to understand more profoundly and to carry out with renewed vigour the mission received by her founder."

The Pope called on the people to refuse to listen to voices which said that truth was less important than personal gain; that comfort, wealth and pleasure were the true aims of life; that the refusal of new life was better than generosity of spirit and the taking up of responsibility; that justice must be achieved but without any personal involvement by the Christian; that violence could be a means to a good end; that unity could be built without giving up hate.

Straight talking to Maynooth Seminarians

Priests, religious and seminarians were given some very straight taking by the Pope at St. Patrick's College, Maynooth, on the Monday.

The Pope made it plain that all in religious life should always remember what they had undertaken.

He emphasised the importance of always looking like priests and nuns and wearing visible signs of their consecrated lives.

"People need signs and reminders of God. In the modern secular city, where there are few reminders of God, you will only help the trend towards taking God off the streets by adopting secular modes of dress and behaviour yourselves."

His words were applauded by the huge crowd of priests, nuns, students and families waiting to see him in the damp, early morning mist of the elegant college grounds.

Speaking first to priests, he said that Christ's work could not be done by the lukewarm or halfhearted. If the people were to be encouraged to keep the Faith, they needed to have the kind of men as priests they expected – holy men with life-styles that bore true witness to Christ. Furthermore, the 1980s could be a decisive period for the faith of Ireland and there could be no complacency.

This plain speaking was greeted with enthusiasm. One priest said: "He is telling us priests that we must make sacrifices too – as we ask lay people to do."

A nun said: "I think that we nuns and priests should always look what we are. But I also think that people should be able to tell that we are religious not only by the clothes we wear but by our lives. I have been a nun for 20 years and always wear my habit."

A 20-year old seminarian from Maynooth agreed that priests should always look like priests, adding that he thought the Pope was a fabulous man who talked a great deal of common sense.

A university student, who had spent the night in wet grass at Maynooth with a large group of students, said: "Young people prefer to know who are priests."

The Pope also criticised some modern, liberal theologians. He warned them that if they taught anything not accepted by the College of Bishops united with the Pope, they were causing confusion among the Faithful.

"This is not a limitation but a liberation: for it preserves them from subservience to changing fashions and binds them securely to the unchanging truth of Christ, the Truth which makes us free."

The main theme of the Pope's speech was the encouragement of those who had undertaken the religious life and a call for more prayers. He said that time must always be found to be with Christ in prayer; priests could become so immersed in the work of the Lord that they rejected the Lord of the work.

At the end of his speech, the Pope relaxed and seized the microphone with the air of a professional entertainer. For the first time he spoke without a script in almost perfect English. "Now," he said in his clear, loud voice, "say to me how many mistakes the Pope make in his speech?"

The crowd were delighted and cheered, singing once again the song that has become almost a modern Papal anthem: *"He's Got the Whole World in his Hands."*

The Pope held up his hand for silence. "I say to you he did two mistakes, surely two mistakes and perhaps more." Following his speech as he delivered it, the only mistake I could hear was the use once of the word 'of' instead of 'for'.

As the Holy Father climbed off the crimson, silk-draped platform, the crowd sang again: "He's Got the Whole World in his Hands". Cheering and clapping broke out as he drove round in the 'Popemobile'. Again, Papal flags were a sea of colour.

The Pope had arrived at Maynooth almost 40 minutes late because bad weather had delayed his helicopter take-off from Dublin. Crowds had been arriving through the night, although it was damp and chilly. As soon as the helicopter touched down the Pope was taken to the chapel, where he greeted Ireland's 1,000 student priests.

The beautiful Gothic building has 454 stalls, the largest number in any church in the world. Nearly 10,000 priests have been ordained there.

The Pope also signed the visitor's book, which contains the signatures of Edward VII, Queen Alexandra, George V and Princess Grace of Monaco.

As soon as he had finished his short speech to the seminarians, the Pope came out into the grounds. Before him in procession came the seminarians in their white cassocks. They stood before the altar.

There was no doubt about the feelings of the students as they came away after this historic morning. One said: "The Pope made it all sound so worthwhile. It was as though he was giving us a pat on the back.

"We are all pretty tired here – we've had about six hours' sleep since the Pope arrived as we have been helping out with giving Communion.

"But it has been worth all the effort. He really is a holy man. He speaks the word of Christ with such conviction and brings it really alive. That man really is just something else."

Limerick: Sanctity of Marriage

The nationwide fiesta which Ireland enjoyed with Pope John Paul II had its last highlight at Greenpark Race Course, Limerick on the Monday, when 400,000 people gathered against a backdrop of trees and a distant view of the Clare Hills across the River Shannon.

The Pope used the occasion to deliver a powerful address, re-affirming the Church's traditional teachings on the sanctity of marriage and the family, and reminded the laity of the challenge of their own vocation.

The address was simple, traditional, but with a freshness and vigour that is so much the style of Pope John Paul.

He called on all to "revere and protect your family and your family life" for it was the place where the laity's "royal priesthood" was chiefly exercised.

He said: "Do not be discouraged, do not follow the trends where a close-knit family is seen as outdated. The Christian family is more important for the Church and for society today than ever before."

Divorce became easier and easier to obtain once it had been introduced and it gradually came to be accepted as a normal part of life.

The Pope starts his drive through the large crowd gathered at Maynooth College.

Pope John Paul II embraces two children who presented him with flowers during the Mass in front of an estimated 400,000 people at Limerick Racecourse.

"The very possibility of divorce in the sphere of civil law makes stable and permanent marriages more difficult for everyone."

He hoped that Ireland would always continue to give witness to her traditional commitment to the sanctity and indissolubility of the marriage bond.

He added: "Marriage must include openness to the gift of children. Generous openness to accept children from God as the gift to their love is the mark of the Christian couple.

"Respect the God-given cycle of life, for this respect is part of our respect for God Himself, Who created male and female, Who created them in His own image, reflecting His own life-giving love in the patterns of their sexual being."

The Pope continued with a plea for an absolute and sacred respect for the sanctity of human life from the first moment of conception.

He said: "To attack unborn life at any moment from its conception is to undermine the whole moral order which is the true guardian of the well-being of man."

He asked young women not to listen to those who told them that working at a secular job and succeeding in a secular profession was more important than the vocation of giving life and caring for that life as a mother.

"The family is the true measure of greatness of a nation, just as the dignity of man is the true measure of a civilisation."

Prayer in the home was another subject dear to the Pope's heart.

He said: "May I express a wish: that every home in Ireland may remain, or begin again to be, a home of daily family prayer. That you would promise me to do this would be the greatest gift you could give me as I leave your hospitable shores."

He warmly commended the pastoral programme planned by the Irish hierarchy to encourage greater sharing by parents in the religious education of their children. Furthermore, he appealed to parents to continue fostering vocations to the priesthood and the religious life among their children.

The Pope spoke at length on the lay vocation.

"Every lay Christian is an extraordinary work of God's grace and is called to the heights of holiness. Sometimes, laymen and women do not seem to appreciate to the full the dignity and the vocation that is theirs as lay people.

"No, there is no such thing as 'ordinary laymen' for all of you have been called to conversion through the death and resurrection of Jesus Christ."

It was their specific vocation and mission to express the Gospel in their lives and thereby to insert the Gospel as a leaven into the reality of the world in which they lived and worked, he said.

There had to be consistency between faith and daily life.

"You cannot be a genuine Christian on Sunday unless you try to be true to Christ's Spirit also in your work, your commercial dealings, at your trade union or your employers' or professional meetings.

"How can you be a true community in Christ at Mass unless you try to think of the welfare of the whole national community when decisions are being taken by your particular sector or group?

"How can you be ready to meet Christ in judgment unless you remember how the poor are affected by the behaviour of your group or by your personal lifestyle?"

So anxious had the Pope been to deliver the whole address and to drive round the crowds at Limerick (something which he had to omit in Knock) that when his tight schedule was running late he sent word that the Mass in Limerick should begin without him. He arrived shortly after the Gospel.

At Shannon Airport, the Pontiff bids farewell to Ireland.

"Man cannot live without love. He remains a being incomprehensible in himself; his life is senseless if love is not revealed to him, if he does not encounter love, if he does not experience it and make it his own, if he does not participate intimately in it. This is why Christ the Redeemer 'fully reveals man to himself' ... this is the human dimension of the mystery of the Redemption ... man finds again the greatness, dignity and value that belongs to his humanity."

"Redemptor Hominis", 1979

"We are all called upon to do everything possible to banish from society not only the tragedy of war but also every violation of human rights, beginning with the indisputable right to life, which every person enjoys from the very moment of conception. The violation of the individual human being's right to life contains the seeds of the extreme violence of war."

World Day of Peace, 1995

"Earthly suffering, when it is accepted in love, is like a bitter nut which encloses the seed of new life, the treasure of divine glory which will be given to man in eternity."

1993

"To save man does not mean only not to kill him, not to mutilate him or not to torture him. It also means giving the hunger and thirst for justice which is in him the possibility of being satisfied. We risk making the victims of the most atrocious deaths die again if we do not have a passion for justice and if we do not commit ourselves, each according to their own ability, to making sure that evil does not prevail over good as happened with millions of sons and daughters of the Jewish people. Efforts to free humanity from every hint of racism, exclusion, margination, enslavement and xenophobia must be doubled."

1994

"The culture of death ... humiliates the individual, not respecting the weakest and frailest creatures, and trying even to undermine the sacred dignity of the family, the heart of society and of the Church."

1994

"There is the risk of an alliance between democracy and ethical relativism, which would remove any sure moral reference point from political and social life ... As history demonstrates, a democracy without values easily turns into open or thinly disguised totalitarianism."

"Veritatis Splendor", 1993

"God's law does not reduce, much less do away with human freedom; rather it protects and promotes that freedom ... Some people, however, disregarding the dependence of human reason on divine wisdom ... have actually posited a complete sovereignty of reason in the domain of moral norms."

"Veritatis Splendor", 1993

"Allow me, dear brothers, to recall the events that occurred 13 years ago in St. Peter's Square. We all remember that afternoon hour when several pistol shots were fired against the Pope with the intention of taking his life. The bullet, which passed through the abdomen, is now at the sanctuary of Fatima; the sash, pierced by the bullet, is at the sanctuary of Jasna Gora. It was a maternal hand that guided the path of the bullet, and the Pope, in agony, was transported to the Gemelli hospital, pausing on the threshold of death."

1994

Words of wisdom

History in the making – UK visit

FRIDAY MAY 28
Gatwick Airport
Victoria Station
Westminster Cathedral
Buckingham Palace
Southwark Cathedral

SATURDAY MAY 29
Digby Stuart College
Canterbury
Wembley Stadium

SUNDAY MAY 30
Crystal Palace
Coventry
Liverpool

MONDAY May 31
Liverpool
Manchester
York
Edinburgh

TUESDAY JUNE 1
Edinburgh
Glasgow

WEDNESDAY JUNE 2
Cardiff
Pontcanna
Cardiff Castle
Ninian Park

(above) The Apostolic Pro-Nuncio, Archbishop Bruno Heim (left) and Bishop Cormac Murphy O'Connor, Bishop of Arundel and Brighton, in whose diocese Gatwick lies, greeted the Pope aboard his plane.
(below) The Duke of Norfolk greets the Pope on his arrival at Gatwick.

The first reigning Pope to visit Britain arrived on the Alitalia plane, *Citta di Siracusa*, in brilliant sunshine at Gatwick Airport just after 8.00am on Friday 28th May, 1982.

Pro-Nuncio Archbishop Bruno Heim and Bishop Murphy-O'Connor of Arundel and Brighton – the diocese in which Gatwick is situated – were first to enter the plane. Seconds later Pope John Paul II appeared, blessing the crowd of 2,500, many of whom had camped out at the airport overnight.

True to form, his first act was a symbolic kissing of the ground and after Cardinal Hume and the Duke of Norfolk had officially welcomed him, the Pope expressed his joyful anticipation and his gratitude for the ecumenical efforts that would take place during this "journey of faith".

He then turned to the issue that had cast a shadow over the preparations for his visit, even at one point putting it in jeopardy – the Falklands crisis.

"My visit," he said, "is taking place at a time of tension and anxiety."

He acknowledged the efforts that had been made to find a diplomatic solution to the crisis and deeply regretted their failure. He spoke of his "serious concern" and of his own efforts to persuade all parties concerned "to avoid violence and bloodshed".

And he thus established the theme of his pastoral visit – reconciliation:

"In a world scarred by hatred and injustice," he said, "and divided by violence and oppression, the Church desires to be a spokesman for the vital task of fostering harmony and unity and of forging new bonds of understanding and brotherhood."

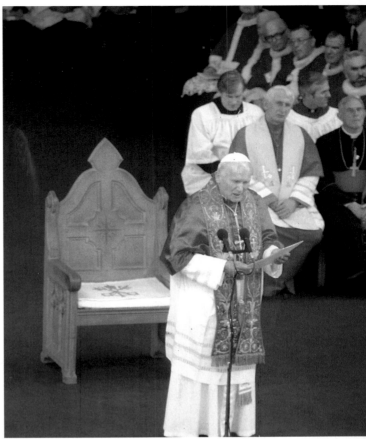

(above) Cardinal Basil Hume listens intently to His Holiness during a service in Westminster Cathedral.

After arriving from Gatwick at Victoria Station, (in the same railway carriage used by the Prince and Princess of Wales to leave for their honeymoon), Pope John Paul II made the short journey to Westminster Cathedral for the first Mass of his visit.

With 3,000 people on the piazza and 1,500 packed inside, the papal procession arrived to strains of *Tu es Petrus*.

In his homily the Pope gave thanks that God had given him the grace of coming amongst us:

"Today, for the first time in history, a Bishop of Rome sets foot on English soil," he said to thunderous applause.

"This fair land, once a distant outpost of the pagan world, has become, through the preaching of the gospel, a beloved and gifted portion of Christ's vineyard.

"Yours is a tradition embedded in the history of Christian civilisation. The roll of your saints and of your great men and women, your treasures of literature and music, your cathedrals and colleges, your rich heritage of parish life speak of a tradition of faith. And it is to the faith of your fathers – living still – that I wish to pay tribute by my visit.

"Christians down the ages often travelled to that city where the Apostles Peter and Paul had died in witness to their faith and were buried. But, during 400 years, the steady flow of English pilgrims to the tombs of the Apostles shrank to a trickle. Rome and your country were estranged. Now the Bishop of Rome comes to you. I truly come at the service of unity in love, but I come as a friend, too, and I am deeply grateful for your welcome."

He continued: "London is particularly proud of two outstanding saints, great men also by the world's standards, contributors to your national heritage, John Fisher and Thomas More.

"John Fisher, the Cambridge scholar of Renaissance learning, became Bishop of Rochester. He is an example to all bishops in his loyalty to the faith and in his devoted attention to the people of his diocese, especially the poor and the sick.

"Thomas More was a model layman living the Gospel to the full. He was a fine scholar and an ornament to his profession, a loving husband and father, humble in prosperity, courageous in adversity, humorous and godly. Together they died, victims of an unhappy age. Today we have the grace, all of us, to proclaim their greatness and to thank God for giving such men to England.

"In this England of fair and generous minds, no one will begrudge the Catholic community pride in its own history. So I speak last of another Christian name, less famous but no less deserving honour. Bishop Richard Challoner guided the Catholics of this London district in the 18th century, at what seemed the lowest point of their fortunes. They were few. It seemed they might well not survive. Yet Bishop Challoner bravely raised his voice to prophesy a better future for his people. And now, two centuries later, I am privileged to stand here and to speak to you, in no triumphal spirit, but as a friend, grateful for your kind welcome and full of love for you all."

After a hectic Friday, the Pope was in Canterbury on Saturday for what was to prove another historic day. Christian unity took a huge step forward on the eve of Pentecost, when for the first time since the Reformation, a Pope and an Archbishop of Canterbury led a joint service of prayer and blessing.

At the service, the Archbishop of Canterbury, Dr. Runcie, said: "I rejoice that the successor of Pope Gregory, who sent St. Augustine, stands here today in the church which is built on their partnership in the gospel."

The Pope, in a 20-minute address, said it was an historic day for which, "centuries and generations had waited".

"I appeal to you in this holy place," he said, "with all my fellow Christians, and especially the members of the Church of England and the members of the Anglican Communion throughout the world, to accept the commitment to which Archbishop Runcie and I pledge ourselves anew before you today."

After the service the two signed a Common Declaration of Unity which set out the steps already taken and the plans for unity in the future.

During the Mass for the Anointing of the Sick at St. George's Cathedral, Southwark, the Pope said how much he had been looking forward to meeting the sick and disabled and that he was able to empathise as "I myself have had a share in suffering and I have known the physical weakness that comes with injury and sickness".

"Dear friends, there is no force or power that can block God's love for you," he said. "Sickness and suffering seem to contradict all that is worthy, all that is desired by man. And yet no disease, no injury, no infirmity can ever deprive you of your dignity as children of God, as brothers and sisters of Jesus Christ.

"By dying on the Cross, Christ showed us how to make sense of our suffering. In His Passion we find the inspiration and strength to turn away from any temptation to resentment and grow through pain into new life.

"Suffering is an invitation to be more like the Son in doing the Father's will. It offers us an opportunity to imitate Christ who died to redeem mankind from sin. Thus, the Father has disposed that suffering can enrich the individual and the whole Church.

"We acknowledge that the Anointing of the Sick is for the benefit of the whole person. We find this point demonstrated in the liturgical texts of the sacramental celebration: 'Make this oil a remedy for all who are anointed with it; heal them in body, in soul and in spirit, and deliver them from every affliction'.

At Coventry

"The anointing is, therefore, a source of strength for both the soul and the body. The prayer of the Church asks that sin and the remnants of sin be taken away. It also implores a restoration of health, but always in order that bodily healing may bring greater union with God through the increase of grace.

"My dear brothers and sisters, as you live the Passion of Christ you strengthen the Church by the witness of your faith. You proclaim by your patience, your endurance and your joy the mystery of Christ's redeeming power. You will find the crucified Lord in the midst of your sickness and suffering.

"As Veronica ministered to Christ on his way to Calvary, so Christians have accepted the care of those in pain and sorrow as privileged opportunities to minister to Christ Himself. I commend and bless all those who work for the sick in hospitals, residential homes and centres of care for the dying. I would like to say to you doctors, nurses, chaplains and all other hospital staff: Yours is a noble vocation. Remember it is Christ to whom you minister in the sufferings of your brothers and sisters.

"I support with all my heart those who recognise and defend the law of God which governs human life. We must never forget that every person, from the moment of conception to the last breath, is a unique child of God and has a right to life. This right should be defended by the attentive care of the medical and nursing professions and by the protection of the law. Every human life is willed by our heavenly Father and is a part of His loving plan.

"Do not turn away from the handicapped and dying"

"No State has the right to contradict moral values which are rooted in the nature of man himself. These values are the precious heritage of civilisation. If society begins to deny the worth of any individual or to subordinate the human person to pragmatic or utilitarian considerations, it begins to destroy the defences that safeguard its own fundamental values.

"Today I make an urgent plea to this nation. Do not neglect your sick and elderly. Do not turn away from the handicapped and dying. Do not push them to the margins of society. For if you do, you will fail to understand that they represent an important truth. The sick, the elderly, the handicapped and the dying teach us that weakness is a creative part of human living, and that suffering can be embraced with no loss of dignity. Without the presence of these people in your midst you might be tempt-

ed to think of health, strength and power as the only important values to be pursued in life. But the wisdom of Christ and the power of Christ are to be seen in the weakness of those who share His sufferings.

"Let us keep the sick and the handicapped at the centre of our lives. Let us treasure them and recognise that we are giving it to them; we end by realising that they have enriched us."

The Knavesmire racecourse in York had never witnessed an event like it. Under the symbol of linked wedding rings, the Pope celebrated a service for the family before over 200,000 people from the north-east of England – the last time the Holy Father was on English soil.

And Pope John Paul was in no doubt as to the significance of the area:

"I am conscious of the history, especially the religious history, of this part of England. I refer to Holy Island where Aidan and Cuthbert brought the Catholic faith. I recall Bede, who wrote so lovingly of the early life of the Church in England. I remember that a thousand years later men and women laid down their lives in this region for the faith they loved. Mary Ward taught the Gospel of Jesus Christ to English exiles; Margaret Clitherow gave her life in this city of York. These holy women inspire women today to take their rightful place in the life of the Church, as befits their equality of rights and particular dignity. In that same period, the priest, Nicholas Postgate, carried the Gospel across the moors and gave his life on this very spot."

"Christian marriage," the Pope said, "is a sacrament of salvation and a pathway of holiness for all family members.

"With all my heart," he said, "I urge that your homes be centres of prayer."

On the subject of mixed marriages, he said: "To these families I say: You live in your marriage the hopes and difficulties of the path to Christian unity. Express that hope in prayer together, in the unity of love. Together invite the Holy Spirit of love into your hearts and into your homes. He will help you to grow in love and understanding."

Whilst pointing out that some marriages fail, he said, "But still it is our duty to proclaim the true plan of God for all married love and to insist on fidelity to that plan, as we go towards the fullness of life in the Kingdom of heaven."

And the Pope concluded with a thought that was never far from his mind during his visit: "And how can we not recall those families – in Britain and in Argentina – who bear the heavy weight of pain and sorrow because of the loss of loved ones in the South Atlantic? As we ask God to comfort them in their affliction, let us pray for peace."

Cheering crowds thronged around the 'Popemobile' at Glasgow's Bellahouston Park. It had been feared that Glasgow, one of the most sectarian-divided cities on his tour, would prove a trouble spot.

As it was, a capacity crowd of over a quarter of a million – one third of Scotland's Catholics – turned out to attend a Mass celebrated by the Pope.

"Of all the expressions of faith," the Pope said in his homily, "none was more spontaneous than that uttered by Andrew, the fisherman of Galilee: 'We have found the Messiah!' (Jn 1:41). So profound was the impression Jesus made upon him at their first encounter that 'early next morning Andrew met his brother and said to him, We have found the Messiah! – which means the Christ – and he took Simon to Jesus. Jesus looked hard at him and said, You are Simon son of John; you are to be called Cephas – meaning Rock' (Jn 1:41-2). It was Andrew, the heavenly patron of your beloved Scotland, who introduced Peter to Jesus!

"Today marks another significant moment in the history of our salvation: the Successor of Peter comes to visit the spiritual children of Andrew! We are bound one to another by a supernatural brotherhood stronger than that of blood. Here and now we testify that we profess that identical faith in Jesus, and we

Thirty-six hours after the FA Cup Final replay (Spurs beat QPR 1-0), the Pope celebrated the first Mass of Pentecost in front of 75,000 people at Wembley.

The first cheer of the afternoon was when the statue of Our Lady of Walsingham appeared from the players' tunnel.

The Holy Father's tightly-organised itinerary would not allow him to visit England's most famous shrine, so the statue came to the Pope.

In his homily, the Pope referred to England as "Our Lady's Dowry", and spoke of her shrine at Walsingham, asking that "your homes be schools of prayer for both parents and children".

"Keep Sunday Holy, go always to Mass; love and respect your bishops," he said.

firmly hope that we too can lead others to Him. This common profession of faith is the compelling motive behind my pastoral visit to your homeland.

"Dearly beloved in Christ! What response has Scotland given in the past to God's invitation? Christian history narrates that from very early times, perhaps even as early as the second half of the fourth century, Scotland embraced the Gospel of Jesus Christ. For over 1,500 years His holy name has been invoked in this land. St. Ninian, St. Columba and St. Kentigern were the first to evangelise the pagans and establish a primitive Christian Church.

"Although situated geographically on the remote edge of Europe, the Church in Scotland became especially dear to the Popes, at the centre and heart of Christianity, and they conferred upon it the exceptional title *Specialis Filia Romanae Ecclesiae*, 'Special Daughter of the Roman Church'! What a magnificent designation!

"The 16th century found the churchmen and the laity unprepared for the religious upheaval of that day, which vehemently swept away the medieval Church from Scotland.

"Even this, however, forms part of God's providence: for the centuries that followed witnessed a valiant struggle for survival in the face of persecution and exile. Who has not heard of St. John Ogilvie, the Jesuit, who – only a few miles from where I now stand – surrendered life itself to witness to the Faith of Christ?

Dear beloved Catholics of Scotland, the prayers of your forefathers did not go unanswered! Their firm hope in divine providence was not disillusioned!

"You are the heirs to the sacred heritage. Your forefathers have

The most fervent crowds yet...

A 300-yard journey along Hope Street took the Pope from the Anglican Cathedral to the Metropolitan Cathedral of Christ the King in Liverpool at the end of day three of his visit.

"Welcome Peter to the very heart of your Liverpool home," said Archbishop Worlock after the Pope had arrived from the Anglican Cathedral where he had been greeted by Bishop Sheppard and the applause of 4,000 Liverpudlians from many churches.

He was delayed on his entrance to the Metropolitan Cathedral by 2,000 young people outside – some of the most fervent crowds of his visit so far.

Referring to the ecumenical efforts, already much in evidence, of Archbishop Worlock and Bishop Sheppard, the Pope said: "The sin of disunity among Christians weighs heavily upon the Church."

Priests ordained in Manchester by the Holy Father

Twelve of the luckiest priests in 1982 were the dozen ordained by the Holy Father in front of 200,000 people in Manchester's Heaton Park.

The Pope urged them to keep up the tradition of visiting parishioners in their homes.

It was, he said a good tradition of the Church in England: "It is a pastoral practice that should not be neglected."

Giving guidelines, he told the ordinands they must develop daily patterns of prayer and penance as a regular part of their lives.

"You must try to deepen every day your friendship with Christ," he said. "You must also learn to share the joys, the sorrows and the frustrations of the people entrusted to your care. Bring to them Christ's saving message of reconciliation.

"The partnership between priest and people is built upon prayer, collaboration and mutual respect and love. That has always been the tradition of these islands. May it never be lost."

handed on to you the only inheritance they really prized, our holy Catholic faith!

"What was a dream a century ago has become the reality of today. A complete transformation of Catholic life has come about in Scotland, with the Catholics of Scotland assuming their legitimate role in every sector of public life and some of them invested with the most important and prestigious offices of this land.

"You originate in the past, but you do not live in the past. You belong to the present and your generation must not be content simply to rest on the laurels won by your grandparents and great-grandparents. You must give your response to Christ's call and follow Him and enter with Him as co-heirs into His Father's heavenly Kingdom. But we find it harder to follow Christ today than appears to have been the case before. Witnessing to Him in modern life means a daily contest, not so quickly and decisively resolved as for the martyrs in the past.

"The spirit of this world would have us capitulate on the most fundamental principles of our Christian life. Today, as never before, the basic doctrines of the Faith are questioned and the value of Christian morality challenged and ridiculed. Things abhorred a generation ago are now inscribed in the statute books of society. Matters of such magnitude demand the fullest attention of our Christian generation, of our Christian conscience.

"To provide the answers to such questions is a daunting task. It would be an impossible challenge for the majority of the faithful to attempt unaided. But you are not alone. The Spirit of God is operative in the Church. Never before as in recent years has the teaching of the Catholic Church been so extensively re-formulated, precisely with the issues that trouble the modern conscience in mind.

"In the name of all the shepherds of Christ's flock, to whom the office of pastors and teachers has been divinely entrusted, I assure you that we are acutely aware of the problems you have to face in life, and of the anxiety which so often fills your hearts.

"Beloved sons and daughters! I have been kept fully informed of the careful preparations, spread over many months, which have preceded my pastoral visit to Scotland. With admiration and satisfaction I have followed the intense programme proposed by the bishops for a spiritual renewal of the Catholic community, to ensure that the effects of my visit produce fruits that will endure. From the depths of my heart I thank each and every one of you for the prayers that have accompanied this preparation, for every effort that has been made to guarantee its success. 'This is the day made memorable by the Lord'."

National Youth Event at Cardiff's Ninian Park
Wild scenes greet the Pope's call to follow Christ

In what was more reminiscent of a pop concert, the young people of England and Wales roared "John Paul, John Paul" as they waited for him to arrive.

When he did arrive, he called for them to launch a crusade of prayer: "It's my hope that as long as the memory of this visit lasts, it may be recorded that John Paul II came to Britain to call you to Christ and to invite you to pray.

"Prayer transforms our individual lives and the life of the world. Young men and women, when you meet Christ in prayer, when you get to know His Gospel and reflect on it in relation to your hopes and your plans for the future then everything is new.

"In prayer, united with Jesus, you begin to breath a new atmosphere. You form new goals and new ideals. In Christ you begin to understand yourself more fully.

"When you are in contact with the Prince of Peace, you understand how totally opposed to His message are violence and terrorism, and hatred and war.

"In Him you experience the full meaning of an interpersonal relationship that is based on generous love."

From Ninian Park, the Holy Father travelled to Rhoose Airport by motorcade. Cardinal Hume bade him farewell with the following words:

"Dear Holy Father, on behalf of the bishops, priests, religious and people of England and Wales, I would like to thank you sincerely, warmly, lovingly for being with us, giving us so much of your time and so much of yourself. This has been a pilgrimage of love. It has been a festival of friendship. You have taught us much, you have inspired us and you have, I would say, without doubt, confirmed our faith.

"Place your lives in the hands of Jesus"

"You have presented us with a charter upon which I believe that the Catholic Church in this country can base its future. In that charter, I for my part would list five points.

"First, you have emphasised the sacramental life of the Church with the Holy Mass at the very centre of it.

"Then, you have given us all a sense of vocation, be we bishop, priest or laity, and you have encouraged the latter to play a full and active part in the Church of God.

"You have given to us, thirdly, the high ideals of family life.

"And fourthly, you have called us again and again to Christian unity. Both in Canterbury Cathedral and in a remarkable manner in the Anglican Cathedral at Liverpool, I believe that you were able to witness the longing that there is in our land for Christian unity.

"And, finally, you have called us to live and work for peace. During this visit there has been, we cannot deny, a shadow, a shadow that hovered over the South Atlantic, and we have been

(below) Mass and baptisms in Westminster Cathedral

"Jesus ... offers to all mankind a new way of life"

distressed that this has been so. We are so pleased that you called us to pray for all those who have suffered as a result of that sad conflict. You have called us to pay attention to the United Nations Disarmament Conference, and we shall support this with our prayers. Yesterday, in Glasgow, you were telling our brethren from other Churches, but it applies to all of us, that 'We must walk together on our pilgrimage,' and you added, Holy Father, 'hand in hand'.

"God has smiled on us in these last days and we are grateful and humble. Thank you so much."

And before boarding the plane that would take him back to Rome, the Holy Father replied with the following address:

"My pastoral visit to the countries of Britain has now come to an end. I came here as a herald of peace, to proclaim a Gospel of peace and a message of reconciliation and love. I came also as a servant – the servant of Jesus Christ, my Saviour; and the servant, too, of the Christian people. As I have travelled round England, Scotland and finally Wales, in fulfilment of my pastoral duty to confirm my brethren, I have sought to remind Catholics of the whole saving activity of Christ, the Redeemer, our Risen Lord. In each of the countries I have also been able to meet and to pray with our brethren from other Christian communities. For those wonderful opportunities and for the friendship and brotherly welcome I have received everywhere, I give praise to God and I thank you all.

"To the civic authorities of the countries and the cities I have visited, I wish to express my deep gratitude. The help, support and co-operation you have given to the Catholic people in your areas, and the way you have made available suitable places for my pastoral visit, have reminded the world of the great blessing of mutual understanding and respect which are a part of the British inheritance. I also wish to thank the police and all those who have been responsible for public order and for the smooth running of the events of these past few days.

"And now, as I prepare to return to Rome, I express once more my good wishes to all the people of Britain, and in particular to Her Majesty the Queen, especially on this, the anniversary of her Coronation. As I leave you, I do so with the prayer that God may bless all the people of these countries. To the people of Wales, among whom I have spent this memorable day, I say: Bendith Duw Arnoch!

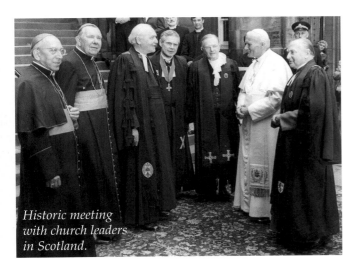

Historic meeting with church leaders in Scotland.

"To all the people of England, Scotland and Wales, I say: May God bless you all. May He make you instruments of His peace, and may the peace of Christ reign in your hearts and in your homes."

Pope John Paul returned to Rome visibly transformed by his visit to Britain. It was reported at the time that the Holy See was astonished by the "whirlwind pilgrimage" and that Karol Wojtyla would "never be the same again".

The Pope himself said after the visit: "I am so very, very happy. Those vibrant young people I met! They are marvellous, marvellous! They are the people of the year 2000 and I love them very much."

At the Vatican, there was an air of awed revelation as if the British had never been quite understood. It was admitted that those historic six days in England, Scotland and Wales moved the Pope more deeply than any of his previous pilgrimages.

A prelate of the Secretariat of State said at the time: "The lack of political profiteering and triumphalism – the 'We've got the Pope and he's on our side!' mentality – and the intensity of sincerity have created profound impressions. All those apprehensions that there would be coolness – how very wrong they were."

And again, a prelate of the Pontifical Social Communications Commission said: "TV close-ups of the Holy Father were studied.

They were quite extraordinary. On his features were observed a serenity and a certain youthful wistfulness.

"He was obviously dreadfully tired, but was sustained by one of the most remarkable collective Christian witnesses he has ever experienced.

"He seemed to be totally at ease, revelling in an atmosphere of genuine Christian joy between pastor and flock."

Elsewhere in the world it was widely reported that the notoriously cynical and critical British press had been only positive.

Speaking on the flight back to Rome, the Pope said: "I am so profoundly happy. It all went far beyond what I expected. They made me feel so sorry to leave them. They made me love them very much. Everyone, everywhere."

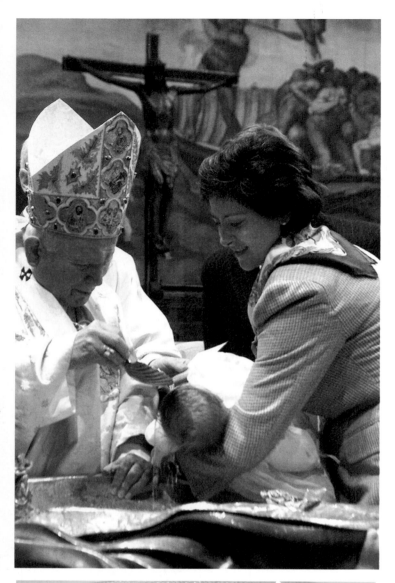

Pope who loved the young

Extracts from Pope's messages to the youth of the world

Message to Young People of Scotland, Murrayfield May 1982
"Your lives cannot be lived in isolation, and even in deciding your future you must always keep in mind your responsibility as Christians towards others. There is no place in your lives for apathy or indifference to the world around you. There is no place in the Church for selfishness. You must show a conscientious concern that the standards of society fit the plan of God. Christ counts on you, so that the effects of his Holy Spirit may radiate from you to others and in that way permeate every aspect of the public and the private sector of national life."

Message for World Day of Peace, 1 January 1996
"I have sought to emphasise strongly the often tragic conditions in which many children are living today. I consider this my duty: They will be the adults of the third millennium. But I have no intention of yielding to pessimism or ignoring the signs of hope.

"How can I fail to mention, for example, the many families in every part of the world in which children grow up in an atmosphere of peace? And how can we not note the efforts being made by so many individuals and organisations to enable children in difficulty to grow up in peace and happiness? Public and private associations, individual families and particular communities have taken initiatives, the only purpose of which is to help children who have suffered some traumatic event to return to a normal life.

"In particular, educational programmes have been developed for encouraging children and young people to use fully their personal talents, in order to become true peacemakers.

"There is also a growing awareness in the international community which, in recent years, despite difficulties and hesitation, has made efforts to deal decisively and systematically with problems connected with childhood.

"The results achieved thus far encourage us to continue these praiseworthy endeavours. If children are properly helped and loved, they themselves can become peacemakers, builders of a world of fraternity and solidarity. With their enthusiasm and youthful idealism, young people can become 'witnesses' and 'teachers' of hope and peace to adults. Lest these possibilities be lost, children should be offered, in a way adapted to their individual needs, every opportunity for a balanced personal growth.

"A peaceful childhood will enable boys and girls to face the future with confidence. Let no-one stifle their joyful enthusiasm and hope!"

Message for World Youth Day, 1996
"To you, young people, I address in particular the call to look toward the epochal frontier of the year 2000, remembering that the future of the world and the Church belongs to the younger generation, to those who, born in this century, will reach maturity in the next."

Blessing to Children, Rome, St. Peter's Square, 14 December 1997
"Christmas is the feast of a Child. It is, therefore, your feast. You await the feast with impatience and prepare for it with joy, counting the days to go until 25 December. I bless you

and children in every part of the world ... May the Baby Jesus fill each child with his joy, especially those who are tried by physical suffering or a lack of affection. Jesus, the source of our peace, is coming."

**Comments during Baptism Mass, Sistine Chapel,
Rome 11 January 1998**
"We thank the Lord for these new creatures and for every new life. Every baby who comes into the world is an 'epiphany' of God, a gift of life, of hope and of joy. In every newly baptised the Church sees its self-renewal together with the gift of life and the wonder of the faith; it sees its perennial reflowering in its sons and daughters and perceives the mystery of salvation which is for all men and women. The celebration of a baby's baptism is a time to renew our decision to keep the flame of faith always lighted in order to become ever more beloved children of the Father."

**Holy Father's Address to University students
attending the UNIV 2000 conference, Rome**
"You need Christ, but Christ also needs you to make him known to your peers, with whom you share experiences and hopes. The Church entrusts you with the mission of bringing them the light of Christ's truth and his universal message of salvation. Always be ready to think of others, forgetting yourselves in order to bring your brothers and sisters closer to God. In this way you will help build a better and more united world, because the conversion and commitment of one are a seed of salvation for all.

"I entrust you, dear young people, and your daily efforts to Mary, Queen of Apostles. Pray to her often and imitate her virtues. She will help you to know Jesus more intimately and to follow him with increasing fidelity and joy."

**Meeting with young people, Plovdiv Cathedral, during
apostolic visit to Azerbaijan and Bulgaria May 2002**
"From the beginning of my service as the Successor of Peter, I have looked to you young people with great care and affection, because I am convinced that youth is not just a time of transition between adolescence and adulthood but a time of life given by God to each person as a gift and a task. It is a time to seek the answer to fundamental questions, like the young man in the Gospel , and to discover not only the meaning of life but also a specific plan of life.

Your personal, professional and social future will depend, dear young people, upon the choices you make in these years: youth is the time to lay foundations; an opportunity not to be missed, because it will never come again! In this moment of your life, the Pope is happy to be with you in order to listen respectfully to your anxieties and cares, your expectations and hopes. He is here among you to share with you the certainty which is Christ, the truth which is Christ, the love which is Christ. The Church looks to you with the greatest care, because she sees in you her own future and she puts her hope in you."

Message to Youth, Rome, 17 March 2005
"I know you are always close to me and never tire of praying for me. I greet you and thank you from my heart ... In an age marked by hatred, selfishness, desires for false happiness, decadent behaviour, the absence of paternal and maternal figures, instability in many young families, we look to you, Jesus in the Eucharist, with renewed hope ... Despite our sins, we trust in your divine mercy. Oh, Jesus in the Eucharist, I entrust to you the young people of Rome, of Lazio and of the whole world, their feelings, affections and plans. Jesus, you who offered yourself to the Father, love them. Jesus, you who offered yourself to the Father, heal the wounds of their spirits."

Religious Reconciliation

Pope John Paul II bows his head at the memorial shrine to St. John the Baptist inside Omayyad Mosque in Damascus, Syria, 6th May, 2001. It was the first time a Catholic pontiff had entered a Muslim place of worship.

Pope John Paul II, seated between Rabbi Elio Toaff and Imam Abdulawahab Hussein Gomaa, attends the "Concert of Reconciliation" at the Vatican on 17th January, 2004. The pontiff called on Jews, Muslims and Christians - "believers in the one God" - to work for "sincere reconciliation" and peace in the world.

Pope John Paul II meets with religious leaders in Baku, Azerbaijan, 23rd May, 2002. On his Holiness' left are Orthodox Bishop Aleksander Iscein and Jewish leader Semyon Ikhiidov. On his right is Sheik Allahshukur Pasha-Zade of the Muslim community. Standing behind the Pope is Cardinal Angelo Sodano, Vatican secretary of state.

Ecumenical Orthodox Patriarch Bartholomew and Pope John Paul II sign a document in the Pope's private library at the Vatican on 1st July, 2004. Members of the Catholic and Orthodox Churches should join in a common witness of the faith against terrorism, religious intolerance and attacks against human life, said the joint statement.

Rabbi Marvin Hier (left), with other members of the Simon Wiesenthal Centre, presents the organisation's 2003 Humanitarian Award to Pope John Paul II at the Vatican on 1st December, 2003. The Jewish human rights group honoured the Pope for his "lifelong friendship" with the Jewish people and his efforts to promote Catholic-Jewish understanding.

Archbishop of Canterbury, Rowan Williams, kisses the hand of Pope John Paul II at the end of their meeting at the Vatican on 4th October, 2003. It was the pontiff's first meeting with the new head of the Anglican Communion.

Pope John Paul II meets with Pope Shenouda II of the ancient Coptic Orthodox church in Cairo on 24th February, 2000. John Paul II was on a three-day pilgrimage to Egypt, where he met with the country's religious leaders.

Hindu holy man, Shankaracharya Madhavananda Saraswati, greets Pope John Paul II at an interreligious meeting in New Delhi, 7th November, 1999.

Pope John Paul II shakes hands with Muslim clerics in Cairo on his way to a meeting with Grand Sheik Mohammed Sayyid Tantawi, 24th February, 2000. The Pope met the Sunni leader just after a meeting with the Pope of the Coptic Orthodox Church in Egypt.

Cardinal Karol Wojtyla (right) walks through the former Nazi prison camp at Auschwitz, in Poland, with Cardinal John J. Krol of Philadelphia and Fr. Walter Ziemba of Orchard Lake, Michigan, after the first government-authorised Mass at the camp on 15th October, 1972. The Mass was held on the anniversary of the beatification of Fr. Maximilian Kolbe.

During his first visit to Poland as pontiff in 1979, Pope John Paul II greets Franciszek Gajowniczek (second from right) at Auschwitz prison camp, who shared a cellblock with St. Maximilian Kolbe but escaped execution at the camp when Fr. Kolbe died in his place. Gajowniczek died on 13th March, 1995, aged 93.

Pope John Paul II reaches out to Holocaust survivor Edith Tziner in the Hall of Remembrance at Yad Vashem in Jerusalem, 23rd March, 2000. Tziner said that as a child in 1945, she was carried out of a Nazi prison camp near Krakow by a young priest, who gave her bread and tea. She realised later that the priest was Karol Wojtyla.

Pope John Paul II kisses the floor of the prison cell of Fr. Maximilian Kolbe at Auschwitz in 1979. The Polish priest, who gave his life in place of a young Jewish father condemned to execution, was declared a saint by the Pope in 1982.

A moment in history

Jordan beckons

by John Thavis

As Pope John Paul II began the first leg of his pilgrimage to the Holy Land on 20th March, 2000, in Jordan, Israel's chief rabbis issued a statement welcoming him with the traditional greeting, "Blessed be your coming to Israel."

"We welcome one who saw fit to express remorse in the name of the Catholic Church for the terrible deeds committed against the Jewish people during the course of the past 2,000 years and even appointed a commission for requesting forgiveness from the Jewish nation with regard to the Holocaust," they said in their statement.

They also welcomed the Pope's recognition of the Jewish "right to return to, and live in, the Holy Land in peace and brotherhood within safe borders."

"From Jerusalem, capital of the State of Israel, and from Zion, the holy city, we pray that we may be granted a good and long life, a life of peace and security, health and peace of mind, a life of human brotherhood," they said.

"May it be his will that the words of the prophet be fulfilled: 'Nation shall not lift up sword against nation, neither shall they learn war any more' (Isaiah 2:4)," the rabbis said.

Shortly after arriving in Amman, Jordan, the Pope made a private visit to the Memorial of Moses monastery on Mount Nebo at Madaba.

Standing on the very mountain where Moses glimpsed the Promised Land, the Pope prayed that peace and justice would come to the peoples of the troubled region.

His face lit by the afternoon sun, he looked out upon a dramatic biblical landscape stretching from the Dead Sea to Galilee.

"Our gaze directed to Jerusalem, let us lift up our prayer to Almighty God for all the peoples living in the lands of the promise: Jews, Muslims and Christians," the Pope said.

"They share the same place of blessing, where the history of salvation has left an indelible trace... Bestow upon all who live here the gift of a true peace, justice and fraternity," he said.

The ruins of a 6th century church which commemorates the place of Moses' death provided a setting for the Pope's stop, about 25 miles southwest of Amman and a few miles from the hill city of Madaba, where thousands of residents cheered as his motorcade passed.

It was the first day of a week-long visit to holy places in Jordan, Israel and the Palestinian territories. The Pope began his jubilee pilgrimage in prayer at the Vatican, since he was unable to visit Iraq, then continued his journey in Egypt, where he visited Mount Sinai and evoked the start of Moses' mission.

On Mount Nebo, the Pope read the biblical account of how Moses led his people for 40 years through the desert before reaching the mountain, where he died before he could enter the

Pope John Paul II takes in the view from Mount Nebo, 20th March 2000. Tradition says Moses first glimpsed the Promised Land from the mountain in Jordan.

pontiff "a symbol of all that is pure and noble in this life."

The Pope, seated at a wooden table inside a temporary pavilion on the tarmac, encouraged the King's efforts to promote tolerance and reconciliation in the Middle East.

"Your majesty, I know how deeply concerned you are for peace in your own land and in the entire region and how important it is for you that all Jordanians – Muslims and Christians – should consider themselves as one people and one family," the Pope said.

He alluded to a 50-year-old problem in Jordan and throughout the region: the great number of Palestinians forced to leave their homes by past wars.

"In this area of the world there are grave and urgent issues of justice, of the rights of peoples and nations, which have to be resolved for the good of all concerned and as a condition for lasting peace," the Pope said.

"No matter how difficult, no matter how long, the process of seeking peace must continue," he said.

The Pope had words of encouragement for his tiny flock of 71,000 Catholics in Jordan, who represent just over one per cent of the population.

He said the Church's attitude of co-operation is embodied in its 85 schools and charitable institutions, open to Muslims and Christians alike.

"The three monotheistic religions count peace, goodness and respect for the human person among their highest values. I earnestly hope that my visit will strengthen the already fruitful Catholic-Muslim dialogue" in Jordan, he said.

The Pope praised the tradition of religious freedom in predominantly Muslim Jordan, which has largely been protected by the country's Hashemite rulers.

He met privately with King Abdullah later in the evening to discuss interreligious dialogue and prospects for Middle East peace.

In his airport speech, the King said the Pope had already brought a light of hope by visiting the region and had served the cause of peace by reminding people of "the virtues of faith and the absolute need for forgiveness of one's enemies."

Three doves symbolising peace were released in front of the pontiff after he stepped off his aeroplane, which was escorted into Jordanian airspace by three fighter planes. Security around the papal motorcade route was heavy and soldiers stood sentry in the bushes around the Mount Nebo church grounds.

Promised Land. The Pope paused before a mosaic cross that marks a possible ancient burial place of the prophet.

A choir of schoolchildren, led by Franciscan nuns and accompanied by a Yamaha electric piano, sang hymns in Arabic and Latin, then chanted "John Paul II, God bless you!" in English. The Pope slowly moved round the various levels of the church, viewing mosaics excavated by Franciscans, including an early scene that depicted Christian symbols of prayer.

Vatican spokesman Joaquin Navarro-Valls said the Pope found Moses a fascinating figure who holds relevance to Christians of every era.

"On Mount Nebo, the Pope wanted to see the Holy Land with the eyes of Moses. But unlike Moses, the Pope intends to reach it," the spokesman said.

Before stepping out onto a mountainside platform to take in the panorama facing Jerusalem, the Pope said he wanted to turn the focus of his pilgrimage towards Christ.

"To him I dedicate every step of this journey I am making to this land, which was his land," he said.

The Pope travelled by car to the mountain plateau shortly after arriving at Amman's Queen Alia Airport, where he appealed for regional peace and interreligious co-operation.

After kissing a bowl of earth, he was warmly welcomed by Jordan's 38-year-old King Abdullah, who called the 79-year-old

Jordan's King Abdullah smiles as Pope John Paul II waves on his arrival in Amman, Jordan, at the start of his historic visit.

A young man presents John Paul II with a bowl of soil from Jordan as he arrives to say Mass in Amman on 20th March.

The two chief rabbis of Israel meet with John Paul II in Jerusalem to exchange views and friendships, 23rd March.

The late Palestinian leader, Yasser Arafat greets Pope John Paul II at the end of Mass in Bethlehem's Manger Square on 22nd March. The Pope told thousands gathered in the square: "Bethlehem is the heart of my jubilee pilgrimage."

(below) John Paul II is flanked by Chief Ashkenazi Rabbi Israel Meir and Muslim cleric Taysir al-Tamini as representatives of the three monotheistic religions met in Jerusalem, 23rd March.

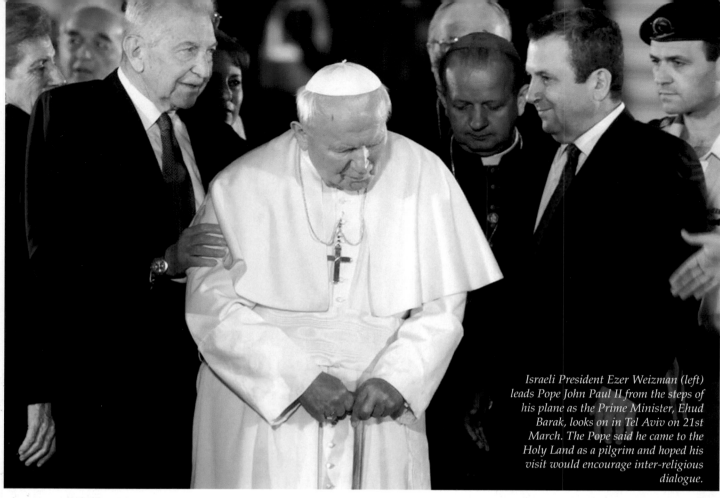

Israeli President Ezer Weizman (left) leads Pope John Paul II from the steps of his plane as the Prime Minister, Ehud Barak, looks on in Tel Aviv on 21st March. The Pope said he came to the Holy Land as a pilgrim and hoped his visit would encourage inter-religious dialogue.

Pope John Paul II kneels and kisses a marble stone at the entrance to the Church of the Holy Sepulchre in Jerusalem, 26th March. The Pope held the last Mass of his Holy Land pilgrimage at the church, traditionally believed to be the place of Jesus' crucifixion, burial and resurrection.

His Holiness peers at the Eternal Flame in the Hall of Remembrance at the Yad Vashem Holocaust memorial in Jerusalem, 23rd March.

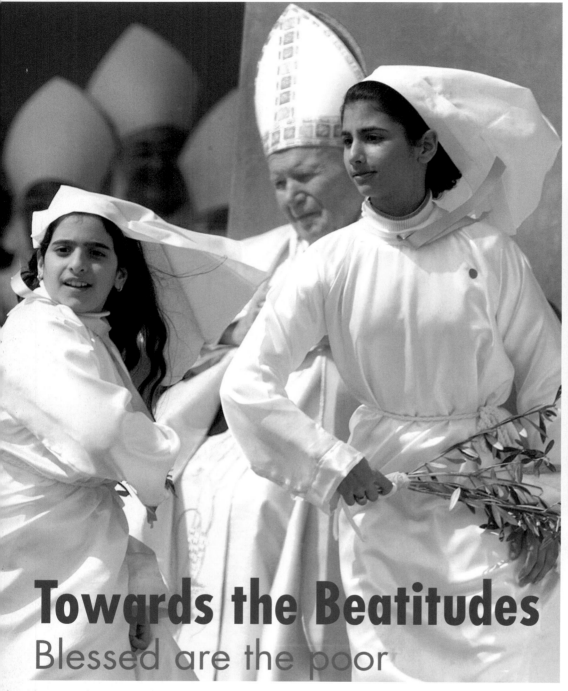

Young Catholic women throw palm branches while Pope John Paul II looks on at the close of an outdoor Mass on the Mount of Beatitudes.

Pope John Paul II sits in front of a large mural depicting Christ the Teacher during Mass on the Mount of Beatitudes. The Pope recalled Christ's Sermon on the Mount during his homily to an estimated 50,000.

Towards the Beatitudes
Blessed are the poor

Pope John Paul II stood on the Mount of Beatitudes and called young people to follow Jesus, confident that the kingdom of heaven can be reached.

The Ten Commandments and the Sermon on the Mount "offer us the road map of our Christian life and a summary of our responsibilities to God and neighbour," the Pope said during the Mass on 24th March.

An estimated 50,000 people, many of them young people from around the world, attended the Mass on the slope of a hill leading down to the Sea of Galilee. Hundreds of them spent the night in huge tents on the lake's eastern shore under a heavy rain shower.

The Mass was delayed for an hour in the hope that the weather would improve whilst the crowd stood in the mud or sat on whatever piece of plastic they could find while dark clouds threatened another downpour.

A strong wind came up during the Mass, and the Pope's zucchetto flew across the altar platform.

Pope John Paul invited the youths to meet Jesus just like the crowds who came to Galilee to see Him 2,000 years earlier,

listened to Him preach the Sermon on the Mount and ate the loaves and fishes He miraculously multiplied.

"In the stillness we hear His gentle and urgent voice, as gentle as this land itself and as urgent as a call to choose between life and death," the Pope said.

Except for the city of Tiberias and the small shrines marking Christian holy sites, most of the Galilean shoreline is undeveloped and large tracts of it are part of a protected nature reserve.

In the early spring, the hillsides were covered with green grass, a sprinkling of red poppies and a generous wash of yellow and purple wild flowers.

"Jesus teaches that the way of love brings the law to fulfilment," the Pope said. "And He taught this enormously important truth on this hill here in Galilee."

"It is strange that Jesus exalts those whom the world generally regards as weak," the Pope said.

"He says to them, 'Blessed are you who seem to be losers, because you are the true winners: The kingdom of heaven is yours'!"

Pope John Paul II rides in his popemobile through the streets of Nazareth after celebrating Mass on 25th March at the Basilica of the Annunciation, seen in the background.

In his master's footsteps
The Sea of Galilee

Near the ancient village of Tabgha, His Holiness prays at the place where Jesus told Peter, "Feed my lambs", 24th March.

For more than 25 years, Pope John Paul II filled the shoes of the fisherman as the 263rd successor of St. Peter. On the fifth day of his Holy Land visit he walked in the footsteps of the first pope near the Sea of Galilee.

On a pilgrimage on 24th March to a string of sites where Jesus chose His disciples and began His preaching life, the Pope had a chance to reflect on the apostle whose combination of strength and weakness long fascinated him.

Near the ancient village of Tabgha, on the shores of a misty Sea of Galilee, the Pope knelt and prayed at the place where Jesus told Peter, "Feed my lambs," instituting papal primacy and apostolic succession.

In Capernaum, a few miles away, the Pope stood next to the ruins of what is traditionally held to be St. Peter's house, where Christ and His disciples would talk for hours after rounds of public preaching.

For the 79-year-old pontiff, it was a visit to the centre of Jesus' activities and to the roots of his own apostolic mission.

At the small Church of the Primacy of St. Peter, the Pope prayed before the massive rock outcrop that stretches across the altar area. Then, hobbling closer, he leaned against the stone and kissed it.

A Franciscan priest read St. John's Gospel, which recounted how the risen Christ appeared to Peter and the other disciples for the last time here, directing them to a miraculous catch of fish. They ate lunch afterwards on the rock, where Christ singled out Peter to lead the church.

So much flowed from this spot for Pope John Paul, who visited here as a bishop in 1963 and took away several rocks from the shore as souvenirs.

Since his election as Pope in 1978, he had strongly affirmed his role as leader of the universal Church, but at the same time invited ecumenical discussion over the future of papal primacy.

Although the Pope cited Peter in later years to illustrate how a pontiff must be willing to make decisions and take some flak, he always saw him as much more than an authority figure.

He spoke frequently of Peter as a man of human weakness and frailty – the man who denied Christ, who showed his limitations and defects, and who protested to Jesus at Capernaum, "I am a sinful man."

Fr. Georges Cottier, the Pope's personal theologian, said at the time that the Pope was absorbed by the paradox in Peter's character, which mixed human weakness and the strength of faith.

"The Pope makes the point that the office [of the papacy] is not tied to the virtue of the person. On the contrary, there's an enormous contrast between Peter's task and human deficiency.

"This is a theme that is very, very dear to the Pope's heart," Fr. Cottier said.

As he aged, the Pope's words about Peter's frailty sometimes took on a more personal dimension.

A few months before the visit, when his declining vigour was especially evident, the Pope made a remark to Vatican officials that many saw as a response to rumours of papal retirement.

"It is with Christ's power that [Peter] could sustain his brethren, despite his own personal weakness ... The man who, as Peter's successor, exercises this ministry can never forget this," the Pope said.

The Pope began his pilgrim's expedition in good form. At one point he climbed some 30 steps to see a chapel that was not even on his itinerary.

He prayed at a church built on the site where Jesus is said to have fed 5,000 people with five loaves and two fish.

In Tabgha, appearing more tired towards the end of the day, the Pope looked out over the moonlit waters of the Sea of Galilee, as Israeli police boats patrolled the shoreline.

Then, held firmly by two aides, he took slow steps up a rain-slickened set of stairs. He might have remembered Christ's words of wisdom to Peter when He picked him to lead the Church:

"When you were younger, you used to dress yourself and go where you wanted; but when you grow old, you will stretch out your hands, and someone else will dress you and lead you where you do not want to go."

In Capernaum, his last stop, the Pope gazed at the stone ruins where Peter is thought to have lived and where the Gospel says Jesus cured the apostle's mother-in-law of a fever.

The city was known as "Jesus' town," and was the place of several early miracles and parables.

There he blessed a statue of St. Peter created by the internationally renowned sculptor, Charles Madden, who told the pontiff that he had made a statue of "our first Pope for our greatest Pope."

The Pope replied, "Thank you, it's beautiful. I love it."

He was presented with a stone from Peter's house, and as he sat in a chair reflecting on the scene, Vatican cardinals accompanying him began singing softly, "Tu es Petrus" ("You are Peter").

Fulfilling a longtime personal desire, Pope John Paul II celebrated Mass at the site said to be where the angel Gabriel announced the conception of Jesus to Mary. "I give thanks to divine providence for making it possible for me to celebrate the feast of the Annunciation in this place, on this day," said the Pope, calling the Mass at the Basilica of the Annunciation on 25th March, "one of the supreme moments of the Great Jubilee of the Year 2000."

As the Pope entered the lower level of the church, where the cave that marks the spot of the Annunciation is located, some 500 invited guests surged forward to greet him. At the cave he knelt, holding on to the altar, to kiss the plaque that commemorates where the "Word was made flesh." He then went to a nearby priedieu and prayed silently for five minutes. At the altar he left a bunch of gold roses in honour of Mary.

The greatest moment
Pontiff places prayer in Wall

by John Thavis

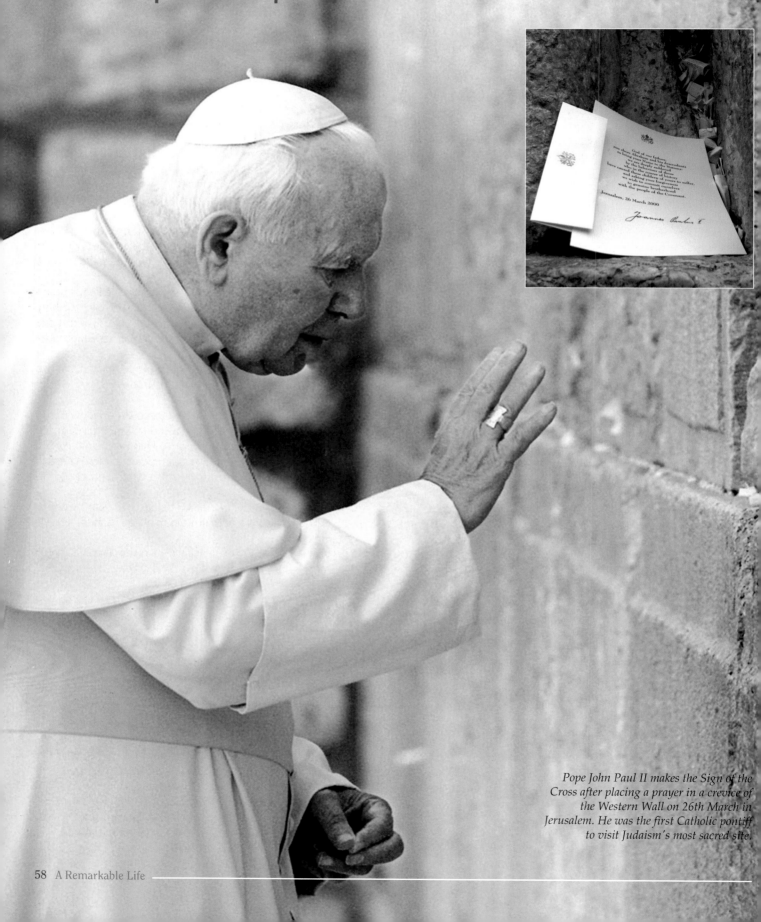

Pope John Paul II makes the Sign of the Cross after placing a prayer in a crevice of the Western Wall on 26th March in Jerusalem. He was the first Catholic pontiff to visit Judaism's most sacred site.

Paying extraordinary visits to Muslim and Jewish holy places, Pope John Paul II became the first pope in history to pray at the Western Wall in Jerusalem, the most sacred place in Judaism, and to visit the al-Aqsa Mosque complex, a centre of Muslim worship.

In a brief but dramatic ceremony on 26th March in Jerusalem's Jewish quarter, the stooped pontiff bowed his head before the wall and quietly pronounced a personal prayer. Then he placed within a crack between the stones a written request for forgiveness for centuries of mistreatment of the Jewish people and traced a blessing with his hand.

As Jews have done for centuries, he placed his trembling hand upon the massive stone blocks of the 2,000-year-old wall, the only remnant of the Second Temple built by Herod the Great and destroyed by the Romans in 70 A.D., when Jews were forced to leave the city.

When he arrived at the site under extremely heavy Israeli security, the Pope stood on a platform and read in Latin the words of Psalm 122, a hymn to Jerusalem, which seemed written for the occasion.

"And now we have set foot within your gates, O Jerusalem," the 79-year-old Pope recited, as a hushed group of Vatican and Jewish leaders sat in the sunlit plaza.

"Pray for the peace of Jerusalem! ... May peace be within your walls, prosperity in your buildings. Because of my relatives and friends, I will say, 'Peace be within you!' Because of the house of the Lord, our God, I will pray for your good," he read.

For centuries, Jews have come to this spot to express their grief at the destruction of their temple and their exile.

That was recalled by Rabbi Michael Melchior, an Israeli minister for diaspora affairs, who greeted the Pope. "Thousands of years of history are looking down on this scene," he said, "and they see you here."

He said the papal visit confirmed the Catholic Church's commitment to "end the era of hatred, humiliation and persecution of the Jewish people."

"In the torturous dungeons of the Inquisition, while awaiting the hangman's noose, when cramped in cattle cars bound for Auschwitz, Treblinka or Majdanek ... Jews have longed for and prayed towards this holy place," the rabbi said.

He also said the time had come on all sides to "end the manipulation of the sanctity of Jerusalem for political gain." While he spoke, an ultra-Orthodox Jew demonstrating against the Pope's visit was dragged out of the plaza by police.

Pope John Paul II places a prayer into a crevice between the stones of the Western Wall during his visit to Judaism's holiest site on 26th March. The Pope prayed at the wall for a few minutes on the final day of his pilgrimage to the Holy Land.

Later, Rabbi Melchior said Jews had a "psychological problem" with the cross he traced in the air when blessing the wall, but "I think that what is important here is not the cross. It's that he touched the wall and the wall touched him."

The 15-minute service at the wall was held after the Pope visited a complex of holy buildings that included the al-Aqsa Mosque, situated on the Temple Mount, just above the Western Wall.

There the Pope met with the Grand Mufti of Jerusalem, Sheik Ikrema Sabri, and said Jerusalem was the common patrimony of Jews, Christians and Muslims.

Vatican officials had been hoping the encounter would help restore inter-religious goodwill after Jewish and Islamic participants traded political accusations at an earlier inter-faith meeting presided over by the Pope a few days earlier.

But the mufti dampened those hopes in an interview published by an Italian newspaper the day before the Pope's visit, in which he said Holocaust death numbers had been exaggerated by Israel in order to gain worldwide sympathy.

The Vatican did not comment directly on the mufti's statements. Two days earlier, the Pope had made a poignant visit to a Holocaust memorial and said of the Nazi attempt to exterminate Jews: "No one can forget or ignore what happened. No one can diminish its scale."

Politics crept into the meeting on Temple Mount when a Palestinian flag was borne aloft by balloons just as the Pope arrived, in defiance of Israeli authorities, who insist the 135-acre walled mount is part of Israel.

The Pope's Muslim hosts seemed eager to enlist the Pope's moral support in their efforts to maintain religious control over the holy area. Sheik Sabri read a list of grievances against Israel, asking the Pope to "stand by justice" and promote the end of "Israeli occupation of Jerusalem."

The sheik later told reporters he hoped the Pope would denounce oppression against Palestinians from his "Vatican palace" after seeing their situation in the Holy Land.

The Pope and the mufti held their talks in the shadow of the Dome of the Rock, which protects an exposed rock revered for many reasons: as the "rock of foundation" from which the creation of the world began, as the site where Abraham prepared to sacrifice Isaac, and, by Muslims, as the place from which Mohammed ascended to heaven.

The written prayer Pope John Paul II left at Jerusalem's Western Wall will now go on display at the museum at Yad Vashem, Israel's Holocaust memorial.

"It was delivered to Yad Vashem and will be on display, as it should be," a museum spokeswoman said on the day after the Pope visited the wall.

The text of the Pope's message read: "God of our fathers, you chose Abraham and his descendants to bring your name to the nations: We are deeply saddened by the behaviour of those who in the course of history have caused these children of yours to suffer, and asking your forgiveness, we wish to commit ourselves to genuine brotherhood with the people of the Covenant. Johannes Paulus II (John Paul II)."

The prayer was the same recited by the Pope at the Vatican on 12th March during a Mass asking God's forgiveness for the sins and faults of Catholics in the past.

The museum spokeswoman said that after the Pope had left the site, Moshe Fogel, the government spokesman, brought photographers up to the wall to take pictures of the papal prayer.

"He said it was important for Yad Vashem to have it, so he spoke to one of the religious authorities who oversee the wall and received permission to give it to us," the museum spokeswoman said.

"Usually," she said, "the prayers are blown away by the wind."

John Paul II reads his breviary at the Grotto of the Nativity in Bethlehem, 22nd March 2000.

Pope John Paul II accepts gift of bread during Mass in Bethlehem's Manger Square on 22 March 2000.

Encyclicals

- *Ecclesia de Eucharistia,* "On the Eucharist in its Relationship to the Church" (April 17, 2003)
- *Fides et Ratio,* "Faith and Reason" (September 14, 1998)
- *Ut Unum Sint,* "On Commitment to Ecumenism" (May 25, 1995)
- *Evangelium Vitae,* "The Gospel of Life" (March 25, 1995)
- *Veritatis Splendor,* "The Splendour of Truth" (August 6, 1993)
- *Centesimus Annus,* "On the Hundredth Anniversary of Rerum Novarum" (May 1, 1991)
- *Redemptoris Missio,* "The Mission of Christ the Redeemer" (December 7, 1990)
- *Sollicitudo Rei Socialis,* "The Social Concerns of the Church" (December 30, 1987)
- *Redemptoris Mater,* "The Mother of the Redeemer" (March 25, 1987)
- *Dominum et Vivificantem,* "On the Holy Spirit in the Life of the Church and the World" (May 18, 1985)
- *Slavorum Apostoli,* "The Apostles of the Slavs" (June 2, 1985)
- *Laborem Exercens,* "On Human Work" (September 14, 1981)
- *Dives in Misericordia,* "Rich in mercy" (November 30, 1980)
- *Redemptor Hominis,* "The Redeemer of Man" (March 4, 1979)

Apostolic Letters

- The Rapid Development (January 24, 2005)
- *Mane nobiscum Domine* (October 7, 2004)
- *Spiritus et Sponsa:* on the 40th anniversary of the Constitution "Sacrosanctum Concilium" on the Sacred Liturgy (December 4, 2003)
- *Rosarium Virginis Mariae,* "The Rosary of the Virgin Mary" on the most Holy Rosary (October 16, 2002)
- *Misericordia Dei* on certain aspects of the celebration of the Sacrament of Penance (May 2, 2002)
- Apostolic Letter to the Catholic People of Hungary for the conclusion of the "Hungarian Millenium" (July 25, 2001)
- On the 1700th Anniversary of the "Baptism of Armenia" (February 17, 2001)
- *Novo Millennio Ineunte,* "At the Beginning of the New Millennium" (January 6, 2001)
- 300th Anniversary of the union of the Greek-Catholic Church of Romania with the Church of Rome (July 20, 2000)
- *Inter Munera Academiarum,* "Among the Functions of Academies" (January 28, 1999)
- *Dies Domini,* "On Keeping the Lord's Day Holy" (May 31, 1998)
- *Divini Amoris Scientia,* "The Science of Divine Love" (October 19, 1997)
- *Laetamur Magnopere,* "We Rejoice Greatly" (August 15 1997)
- *Operosam Diem,* "The Laborious Day" (December 1, 1996)
- Apostolic Letter for the 350 Years of the Union of Uzhorod (April 18, 1996)
- Apostolic Letter for the Fourth Centenary of the Union of Brest (November 12, 1995)
- *Orientale Lumen,* "The Light of the East" (May 2, 1995)

- *Tertio Millennio Adveniente,* "With the Coming of the Third Millennium" (November 10, 1994)
- *Ordinatio Sacerdotalis,* "On Reserving Priestly Ordination to Men" (May 22, 1994)
- Apostolic Letter for the organisation of the ecclesiastical jurisdictions in Poland (March 25, 1992)
- Apostolic Letter for the Fifth Centenary of the Evangelisation of the New World (June 29, 1990)
- Apostolic Letter for the Centenary of the 'Opera di San Pietro Apostolo' (October 1, 1989)
- Apostolic Letter on the Situation in Lebanon (September 7, 1989)
- Apostolic Letter on the Occasion of the Fiftieth Anniversary of the Beginning of World War II (August 27, 1989)
- *Vicesimus Quintus Annus,* "The Twenty-Fifth Year" (December 4, 1988)
- *Mulieris Dignitatem,* "On the Dignity and Vocation of Women" (August 15, 1988)
- *Euntes in Mundum Universum,* "Go into the Entire World" (January 25, 1988)
- *Duodecimum Saeculum,* "The Twelfth Century" (December 4, 1987)
- *Spiritus Domini,* "The Spirit of the Lord" (August 1, 1987)
- *Sescentesima Anniversaria,* "The Sixth Hundredth Anniversary" (June 5, 1987)
- *Augustinum Hipponensem* "Augustine of Hippo" (August 28, 1986)
- *Dilecti Amici,* "Dear Friends" (March 31, 1985)
- *Les Grands Mystères,* "The Great Mysteries" (May 1, 1984)
- *Redemptionis Anno* "The Year of Redemption" (April 20, 1984)
- *Salvifici Doloris,* "On the Christian meaning of Human Suffering" (February 11, 1984)
- *A Concilio Constantinopolitano I,* "From the Council of Constantinople" (March 25, 1981)
- *Egregiae Virtutis,* "Of Wondrous Virtue" (December 31, 1980)
- *Sanctorum Altrix,* "The Sustainer of Saints" (July 11, 1980)
- *Amantissima Providentia* "The Most Beloved Providence" (April 29, 1980)
- *Patres Ecclesiae,* "The Fathers of the Church" (January 2, 1980)
- *Rutilans Agmen,* "The Shining Throng" (May 8, 1979)

Apostolic Exhortations
- *Pastores gregis* (October 16, 2003)
- *Ecclesia in Europa,* (June 28, 2003)
- *Ecclesia in Oceania,* (November 22, 2001)
- *Ecclesia in Asia,* (November 6, 1999)
- *Ecclesia in America* (January 22, 1999)
- A New Hope for Lebanon (May 10, 1997)
- *Vita Consecrata,* "The Consecrated Life" (March 25, 1996)
- *Ecclesia in Africa* (September 14, 1995)
- *Pastores Dabo Vobis,* "I Will Give You Shepherds" (March 25, 1992)
- *Redemptoris Custos,* "The Guardian of the Redeemer" (August 15, 1989)
- *Christifideles Laici,* "On the Lay Faithful in the Church and in the World" (December 30, 1988)
- *Reconciliatio et Paenitentia,* "Reconciliation and Penance" (December 2, 1984)
- *Redemptionis Donum,* "The Gift of Redemption" (March 25, 1984)
- *Familiaris Consortio,* "On the Role of the Christian Family in the Modern World" (November 22, 1981)
- *Catechesi Tradendae,* "On Catechesis in Our Time" (October 16, 1979)

Apostolic Constitutions
- *Ecclesia in Urbe,* "The Church in the City" (January 1, 1998)
- *Universi Dominici Gregis,* "Shepherd of the Lord's Whole Flock" (February 22, 1996)
- *Fidei Depositum,* "Guarding the Deposit of Faith" (October 11, 1992)
- *Ex Corde Ecclesiae,* "Born From the Heart of the Church" (August 15, 1990)
- *Pastor Bonus,* "The Good Shepherd" (June 28 1988)
- *Spirituali militum curae* (April 21, 1986)
- *Divinus Perfectionis Magister,* "The Divine Teacher of Perfection" (January 25, 1983)
- Sacrae Disciplinae Leges, promulgates the revised Code of Canon Law (January 25, 1983)
- *Magnum Matrimonii Sacramentum,* "The Great Sacrament of Matrimony" (October 7, 1982)
- *Sapienta Christiana,* "Christian Wisdom" (April 15, 1979)